# NIMA
*A Sherpa in Connecticut*

# NIMA
## *A Sherpa in Connecticut*

**ELIZABETH FULLER**

*illustrated with photographs*

DODD, MEAD & COMPANY

*New York*

Published by Dodd, Mead & Company, Inc.
79 Madison Avenue, New York, N.Y. 10016
Distributed in Canada by
McClelland and Stewart Limited, Toronto

Manufactured in the United States of America
First Edition

*Library of Congress Cataloging in Publication Data*

Fuller, Elizabeth, 1946–
  Nima: a Sherpa in Connecticut.

  1. Nima.  2. Connecticut—Description and travel.
3. Sherpas—Biography.  I. Title.
DS493.9.S5N553  1984    974.6'043'0924    83-25511
ISBN 0-396-8304-8

*To Nima Dorje, Sherpa*

# ACKNOWLEDGMENTS

IT IS IMPOSSIBLE to thank everyone who helped with this book, but I would like to give special thanks to Sue Adler and Kathy McAuliff, Nima's first aid instructors; Dr. Robert Altbaum, Nima's doctor; Mr. Ray Tata, director of Continuing Education at Staples High School; Mr. Anthony Mastroberadino, Nima's English teacher; Robin and Wendy Marston, and Bobby Chettri, of the Mountain Travel Office in Kathmandu. Also, Dr. Slade Wilson; Grover, Kerrie, and Geoffrey Mills; Arlene Skutch; Don, Sally, and Nancy Blinn; Ann, David, and Penny Tolson; Judd Fuller; Lois Krieger, for her patient editing. Also, for the cover photo of Mount Everest and several others in the text, I'm most grateful to Lindley K. Volkwein; and last but not least Pasang and Mingma of Mountain Travel and the Solu Khumbu.

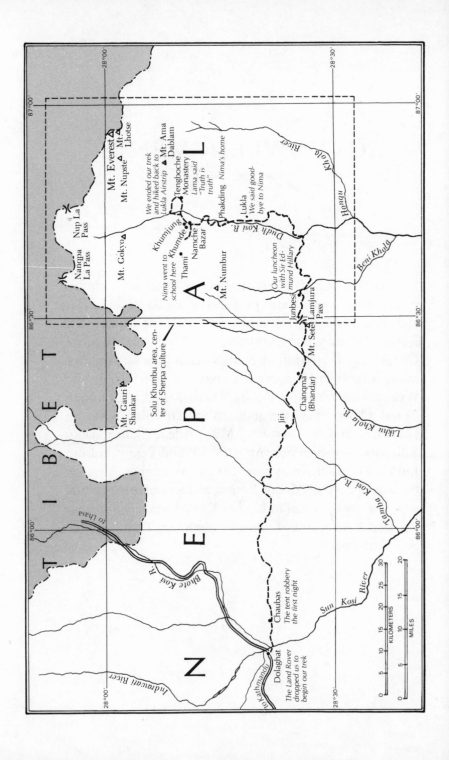

# ONE

NIMA DORJE WAS A SHERPA, born and bred in the shadow of Mount Everest. At two, he helped his mother pick potatoes. At five, he herded yaks with his father. At seven, he crossed the Langpa Pass into Tibet to trade the potatoes. At eleven, he was hired for a British expedition on Mount Everest. Nima climbed to only fourteen thousand feet because he had no shoes. At fourteen, he got his first pair of shoes and trained as a Sherpa guide. At sixteen, he would be an Ice-Fall porter on an assault on Everest, carrying forty-five pounds to twenty-four thousand feet. But at eighteen his life would take a dramatic turn. He would suddenly find himself glued to a color television set in Weston, Connecticut, U.S.A.

On a cool summer day in August of 1979, ten thousand feet up in the small Himalayan village of Phakding, Nima prepared to leave his mountain home of eighteen years. He bowed *namaste* to his mother, father, two sisters, and brother. He filled his red backpack with his other pair of trousers, one sweater, a light blanket, and three gifts and began the ten-day descent to Kathmandu. On arrival he went directly to the office of Mountain Travel, the expedition outfitters he worked for. Here he said "Namaste" to all his Sherpa friends and to his boss, Lhakpa, and picked up an envelope that was marked NIMA DORJE SHERPA. Inside was an Air India ticket that would take Nima halfway around the world to the strange and mysterious land known as Connecticut.

Twelve thousand miles away in Weston, my husband, John, and I waited for word on Nima. We hadn't seen him since we waved good-bye at a tiny dirt landing strip on the precarious edge of a mountain near the Himalayan village of Lukla. That moment marked the end of our forty-day trek through which Nima had mothered and guided us. Now, after six months of red tape, we would be greeting him again. The cablegram read: NIMA NOW ARRIVING JFK AIRPORT AI 103 11 SEP 1535 HOURS MOUNTAIN TRAVEL.

At noon on September 11, John and I drove the hour and a half to Kennedy Airport. As we crossed the Connecticut state line into New York, I was hit with an uncomfortable feeling. I suddenly couldn't remember exactly what Nima looked like. I seemed to recall him looking Japanese, even though Sherpas are of Tibetan stock. But John said he thought Nima looked more like a cross between an American Indian and an Eskimo. Though I couldn't get a clear picture of Nima's face, I did remember how Nima had bowed solemnly to us when we first met him and how we had bowed back.

It was on a chilly March day in Kathmandu, just before we left for our long mountain trek toward the base of Mount Everest. I remembered my first impression—a broad smile, bright white teeth, and mocha-colored skin, capped by shiny black hair. He had looked somewhat frail compared to the other Sherpas. But there was a reason. Nima, like many Sherpas, had contracted tuberculosis. During the weeks of our trek he had gotten visibly worse. John and I felt helpless. The medical resources available in Nepal were meager and inadequate.

During those forty days on the rough Himalayan trail, we grew to love Nima. Not only did he help us over the boulders and along the mountain ledges, but he helped us look at ourselves in an entirely new light. By the time we were ready to say good-bye we found ourselves as attached to Nima as if he were our son. We also found ourselves arranging for him to visit us in the United States. We were sure that proper medical attention could change his future. And the future was now.

As we parked the car, I tortured myself with wild thoughts of Nima disembarking in New York with a planeful of Sherpas. And if John and I couldn't agree on what Nima looked like, how would he recognize us, mixed in with a sea of American faces? Nima had once told us that he thought all Americans looked alike. John reminded me that only a handful of Sherpas have ever visited this country—the most famous of whom was Tenzing Norkay, the first man to reach the top of Everest, with Sir Edmund Hillary.

Nevertheless, as soon as we got inside the terminal I told the Air India ticket agent of my fears and he offered to board the plane personally, locate Nima, help him clear immigration, and deliver him to us.

The electronic Air India arrival board was flashing the news that Flight 103 from London was on the ground. The agent kept his promise. He told John and me where to wait for Nima, and then he left to board the plane and help him clear immigration.

It seemed like forever, waiting for those steel doors from immigration to open. Occasionally, a customs official would walk through, but there was no sign of any passengers coming off Flight 103. Suddenly throngs of people poured through. John scanned one side of the double doors, while I checked the other. We watched closely, just in case the agent had missed Nima. The crowd thinned out as quickly as it had started. Still there was no sign of Nima.

My fears of Nima not being on the flight were beginning to return when we saw the agent coming toward us. He was carrying a red rucksack over his shoulder. Hooked around one arm was a very frail-looking passenger. From a distance, I couldn't be sure if it was a feeble old man or a sick twelve-year-old child. The passenger was so wobbly that I wondered how he had ever survived the trip.

As they approached, I knew this person in the brown baggy pants, plaid shirt, and baseball cap was no stranger. It was Nima. But not the Nima we had known. Not the Nima who carried forty-five pounds to twenty-four thousand feet on Mount Everest. Not the Nima who never walked when he could run. I was so shocked at the sight of what had happened to Nima in just a few short months that I felt as if my body wouldn't carry me toward him. John walked ahead of me. He bowed namaste. Nima's bright face was gone. His eyes were sunken. His cheeks were hollowed out. He smiled wanly. He held up one hand and kept the other hooked onto the agent for balance while he said, "Namaste."

Nothing was how I had imagined it would be. There was none of the joking that there had been back in the Himalayas. I felt as if I didn't know this person. Seeing him half standing, half leaning, as bony as a living skeleton, made me want to run away from him and at the same time grab onto him and tell him that we'd take care of him, that we wouldn't let him die. But I did neither. I stood numbly beside John and bowed namaste. John relieved the agent of Nima's backpack. I took hold of one of Nima's fragile arms, John took the other, and we shuffled to the car.

It was a long drive back to Westport. Nima appeared so pathetic and weak that it hurt to look at him. His head, too heavy for his pencil-thin neck, kept flopping from side to side as he slept fitfully in the car. At intervals, when Nima was awake, John and I asked him questions. We wanted to know how his health could have slipped so rapidly in just six months. But our efforts were futile. Even if Nima had understood what we were getting at, he was too disoriented to communicate anything to us. After several tries we gave up.

In between Nima's naps, John and I took turns pointing out various sights along the Connecticut Thruway. Nima feebly acknowledged the cement scenery with two-word phrases. "Many car . . ." "many people . . ." "many house." For the first time since we had begun making arrangements for Nima's arrival, I was seized with the uncomfortable realization that Nima would not only require our constant attention, but immediate medical treatment as well. The first thing in the morning I would call Dr. Altbaum's office in Westport for an appointment.

Three hours after we had set out for Kennedy we were back in our driveway. Nima seemed to have gained a little strength from his nap in the car; at least enough to inch along behind John as they wound through various rooms on the way to Nima's. Nima politely commented on everything. He gingerly touched the old barnwood paneling as he passed the kitchen and said, "Good wood." He did the same for the chairs, tables, rugs, and everything else he was familiar with.

While John went out to the car to bring in Nima's backpack, I turned on the outdoor lights and opened the sliding glass door that leads out to the deck. Nima stepped out, a little shaky. He appeared to be studying the backyard and river. Seeing no animals grazing, he asked if they were all asleep underneath the house. Every good Sherpa house has an abundance of livestock on the first floor.

It hadn't occurred to me that during the entire time we

spent with Nima in the Himalayas, we had never told him any details about how we lived in Connecticut. Although Nima knew that John wrote books, he probably assumed that that was his hobby, and like every respectable Sherpa, John made his living at animal husbandry and trading.

The tour ended in Nima's room, which up until a year before had been John's office. Nima reacted to seeing his room for the first time by not reacting. He stood at the doorway and looked in, almost as if he were viewing a museum display. John and I were already well inside the room, pointing out the mountain posters, closet, book-shelves, and desk. But Nima stood frozen like a frightened deer. John gently took his arm and led him to the sofa. I turned on the color TV to break the awkward silence. But Nima didn't seem to be the least bit interested in the show. Instead he just stared and said, "Good box, good color." Then he picked up one of the pillows at his side and began studying the weave. The fact that the pillow had a zipper along the seam added immensely to his interest.

I couldn't believe Nima preferred a pillow when he was facing his first TV set, one of the most profound innovations of the twentieth century. Then I had second thoughts. One of those game shows was on the air, the kind where a guy in a banana suit was trying to make a deal with a lady dressed as a carrot.

I went into the kitchen to prepare dinner, and John showed Nima his bathroom. On seeing the toilet, Nima didn't waste time telling John that he had used one before, and he flushed it two times to prove that he really had. But when John asked Nima if he would like to take a shower before dinner, Nima declined, explaining that it was too much trouble for Memsahib. A shower in the Himalayas, if one is lucky enough to find one, is not based on quite the same plumbing principles as the ones we know.

When Nima had been our guide, he knew that John and I couldn't bring ourselves to take even a sponge bath in the raging cold Dudh Khosi River. As a surprise, he steered us to a small village where he knew the family that operated a shower. The shower was on the ground floor, separated from the animals by slats of wood on two sides and sackcloth on the other two. What made this a shower stall was not the dirt-and-dung floor, the sackcloth, or the wood, but rather a small hole in the ceiling about the size of a teacup. There were no nozzles, faucets, or magic massaging shower heads. There was just a good-natured Sherpa who, for five rupees, was more than willing to heat up a huge caldron of water, run up the stairs, and dribble it through the hole.

Now, John had to reassure Nima that he could take a shower without putting us through such rigor. When John turned on the faucets to demonstrate, Nima, startled at the sudden force of the water, jumped back. But after he felt the warm water he decided that a shower might be a good idea. John pointed out the medicine chest, stocked with toothpaste, shampoo, and soap. There was even aftershave, although Sherpas don't need to shave, having only a faint trace of a mustache. And Nima didn't even have that much: he had the skin of a twelve-year-old boy.

Before John left Nima to his shower, he opened up the sleeper sofa and arranged the pillows and blankets on the bed. Then he handed Nima a pair of new flannel pajamas, a terrycloth robe, and slippers to put on after his shower. Nima accepted the new clothes, but he was so exhausted from this strange new country that he didn't have the energy to inspect them as he had the pillow. He did, however, press both palms together in front of his face and bow namaste.

A half-hour went by, and there was no sound of Nima taking a shower. I thought he might be unpacking, but I didn't see how it could take thirty minutes to unload one backpack. We waited another ten minutes, just in case he was in the bathroom. When we still heard no sound, and nearly forty-five minutes had gone by, John knocked on the door. But there was no answer. John knocked again, this time louder. But there was still no answer. We opened the door, and there was Nima sprawled out across the bed. He was sound asleep. His clothes were still on. John put the blanket across his thin body, and I took off his shoes.

As I headed out the door, I noticed that Nima had something clutched in his hand. It was the Polaroid picture that we had taken of Nima and his family back in the Himalayas. John gently opened his hand, carefully removed the worn photo, and placed it on his dresser.

At nine o'clock the next morning, I phoned Dr. Altbaum's office and explained as much as I could to the nurse. I think just the mere suggestion that Nima had TB qualified as an emergency. An appointment was set up for one-thirty that afternoon.

Now that I was well rested and could think more clearly, all sorts of thoughts haunted me. What if Nima's health certificate was wrong and he really did have contagious TB? Would our house be contaminated? Would we be quarantined? What would our friends and neighbors say about our bringing a contagious person to Weston? Or worse, what if we started an epidemic? I had never known anyone who had TB. In fact, my knowledge of tuberculosis was limited to eighteenth-century novels where whole towns were wiped out by an epidemic. Or maybe that was smallpox. However, we *had* been reassured that the doctor in Kathmandu who certified Nima was competent, and that Nima was not in a contagious state.

Our friends were anxious to meet Nima, but they had certain reservations. Everyone we knew, and a few we didn't, warned us about bringing a boy who had never been out of the Himalayas to the Westport-Weston area. John and I took their words of caution in stride. They could not possibly understand, without actually meeting Nima, that he wasn't the type of person who could be contaminated by the Western world. That we were confident of.

By ten-thirty that morning, there was still no sign of Nima stirring. John decided that we should give him until noon. If he wasn't up by then, we would wake him. He had already gone without dinner, and now breakfast. He couldn't afford to miss lunch.

I had intended to take Nima shopping the moment he arrived. He was crazy about American blue jeans. Before we had left the Himalayas, I promised Nima that as soon as I returned home I was going to a store that sold nothing but jeans, and I would send him two pairs. I wasn't quite sure that Nima really believed we had stores that sold *nothing* but blue jeans.

He would ask me, "Jean store have rice?"

"No, Nima," I would say. "Only blue jeans. Nothing else."

That seemed to satisfy him, until he gave it more thought. Then he would try to catch me off.

"Memsahib, store have egg?"

"Nope. No eggs. Only jeans."

"Store have chicken?"

"No chicken. Just jeans."

It seemed that Nima got as much pleasure from questioning me as he did from the thought of an entire store that sold only blue jeans.

Remembering this conversation, John suggested that before Nima got up, I go into Westport and pick up the jeans, a T-shirt, and a sweater for his doctor's appointment, and—even more important—to help boost his spirits. When I got back home around noon, Nima was sitting on a kitchen barstool, making a halfhearted attempt at eating a plate of scrambled eggs and toast. John was facing Nima from the other side of the bar, showing him some of the photos we had taken in the Himalayas.

Nima saw me come in. He smiled, bowed namaste, slowly got down from the barstool, and shuffled toward his bedroom. If Nima had had wrinkles and white hair, he would have looked like a rickety old man. Several moments later, he came back out carrying three packages, each one wrapped in brown rice paper.

Nima bowed from his waist and held out one of the packages to me. It was a Tibetan wool jacket with a simple geometric design over unbleached wool. I fumbled around for the right words to express how beautiful I thought the jacket was. "Good jacket, Nima! Good color, good size, good wool. Namaste." From the expression on Nima's face those words weren't necessary. Nima *knew* the jacket was exquisite, and that anyone in his right mind would love it.

Next, he handed John a package and me another. Inside were two delicately hand-looped miniature Tibetan rugs. Just the thought of how hard he had to work for his money made us feel queasy about accepting the gifts. Sherpa guides make only twenty-five rupees a day, about two dollars and fifty cents. In Nepal, however, that is considered good pay.

While I was trying on my jacket and John was gently brushing the rug with his hand, Nima began telling us how his father had brought the gifts back from a recent yak caravan into Tibet. Nima said he had asked his father to get a colorful jacket, because my North Face parka was all the same color. Nima added that the new jacket should be saved for "wedding and Mani Rimdu time." Mani-rimdu, he said, was a four-day Buddhist festival in which the participants gained merit for the next life while enjoying themselves.

We set off for the doctor's office with Nima dressed in his new jeans, sweater, and red T-shirt. His hair, no longer wet from the shower, hung unevenly over his eyebrows and across the bridge of his nose. He looked so small and vulnerable that I couldn't help but feel responsible for whatever happened to him.

In the car there was that uncomfortable silence that hangs over people who suddenly find themselves in a position to talk but with nothing to say. Finally, I repeated what John had told Nima as we left the house. "Nima, the doctor is very, very good. He is going to help you get strong again."

Nima nodded. His eyes were focused straight ahead. Then he spoke. "Is doctor same like New Zealand doctor? Is doctor same like Spirit A-Tutu?"

Spirit A-Tutu was the tribal doctor of the village of Khumjung. With his drums and yak-butter lamps, he was highly respected by all the villagers. It took me a few seconds to register what Nima meant. The thought of Dr. Altbaum standing in his sterile Westport office, wearing a headdress and beating a tom-tom, was almost too much to visualize.

I looked over at Nima. He was patiently waiting for my answer.

"Nima," I said, "Dr. Altbaum is like the New Zealand doctor. He's not like Spirit A-Tutu."

Had Nima been in good health, I would have elaborated. I decided instead to change the subject.

"Nima, how did you ever walk from your home in the Solu Khumbu to Kathmandu, being so sick?"

"Nima walk many days. Many tired. Many stop. Many sleeps."

The pathetic picture of Nima leaving his home and trekking all the way to Kathmandu was heartbreaking.

"Nima, what did your mother say about you coming to America?"

Nima didn't answer. I thought he might not have understood the question, so I repeated it.

"Mother say Nima lucky boy."

I started to ask Nima another question along that line, but I noticed a tear trickling down his cheek.

"Nima, what's wrong?" I asked. "Are you afraid of going to the doctor?"

Nima didn't answer. He turned his head so that I wouldn't notice the tear.

"Nima," I said, "please tell me what's wrong."

After several moments Nima wiped his face with the sleeve of his new sweater and spoke. "Mother say to Nima, 'No go America. Nima go Khumbu doctor.'"

"Nima, why did she say that?" I really didn't have to ask. It was perfectly logical for her not to want her son to go to a faraway country in his weakened condition. His mother knew that there was a New Zealand doctor at the Khumbu medical station and that Spirit A-Tutu was right there in Khumjung. But what she didn't know was that Nima's condition had been treated in Nepal as much as possible, and that he still wasn't getting any better.

"Mother say, 'Nima go America, Nima die. Nima no come home. Nima no see mother again.'"

"Of course, you'll see your family," I said. "You're first going to get well, and then learn better English and first aid, and then go back a very healthy, smart boy."

"Nima mother very, very old. Mother say, 'Nima go America—mother die.'"

Now I was really confused. "Nima, is your mother sick?"

"No. Mother old. Mother scared *she* die if Nima go."

12

"But you didn't listen to your mother. You came anyway?"

"Nima no listen. Nima go America. Mother scared Nima die. Nima scared mother die. Mother scared . . ."

It sounded as if Nima's mother didn't want him to leave her, sick or not sick. And if that was the case, she was laying on Nima a classic guilt trip to keep him home with her.

Although I was sorry for having upset Nima, sharing his anxieties with me seemed to have made him feel better. In fact, on the way into the doctor's office he managed a smile and said that the doctor had a "good house."

Nima and I went up to the large sliding glass window. I spoke as softly as I could through a slit. "Nima Dorje here for a one-thirty appointment with Dr. Altbaum."

The nurse looked from Nima to me and asked, I thought a little too loudly, what we were there for. Before I had a chance to answer, another nurse came up to her. Whatever the other nurse said motivated her to get up quickly from the low desk and suddenly appear at the doorway leading to the doctor's examining rooms.

The nurse told me to have a seat and Dr. Altbaum would see Nima right away. Nima began to follow her, but before he got to the door, he stopped. The nurse was holding the door open. Nima reached down, took off one beat-up sneaker, and pulled out a handful of crumpled rupees and dollars. He handed them to me and said, "Memsahib, money to pay doctor."

John and I had already agreed that to prevent Nima from feeling as if he were a financial burden we would tell him that medical care in this country is free. But this certainly wasn't the time or place to explain. I took the money, slipped it in my blazer, and felt the eyes of all those waiting taking in this rather unlikely transaction.

I don't know exactly how long I sat in the waiting room,

aimlessly leafing through worn copies of *Golf Digest, Medical Economics,* and *U.S. News & World Report.* I was barely skimming them. At one point I thought I had recognized a neighbor to my right. I was praying that she wouldn't start talking to me and ask what I was there for. I certainly didn't need it spread all over the neighborhood that we were housing a victim of TB.

Aside from the horrifying thought that Nima's certification of noncontagion might be wrong, what kept racing through my mind was that Nima had dropped from a healthy 125 pounds to what looked like 80 or 90 within a few months. What if he were dying and we could do nothing about it? How would we tell his family? Would they ever forgive us?

It was at least forty-five minutes before I saw Dr. Altbaum through that wide glass window where his nurses were working. He didn't even glance out toward me. His face was solemn. He spoke quickly to one of the nurses, then turned and moved out of sight again. The sliding glass window was closed, and I hadn't heard a word he had said.

I put down my magazines and stared directly at the door that sooner or later had to open to bring news of Nima's fate. By the time the nurse finally came through that door I had steeled myself for the worst. I followed her down the antiseptic corridor, feeling weak and without any control in the situation. There was nothing I could possibly do or say to change what I felt was coming. I hated myself for it, but I was thinking that John and I should have not brought Nima to this country.

The door to Dr. Altbaum's examining room was partially open. The nurse motioned for me to wait at the doorway until the doctor was finished with Nima. Nima was sitting slumped-shouldered on the edge of the examining table.

With his shirt off, he reminded me of one of those skeleton cutouts that you hang up at Halloween.

Nima saw me, smiled, and then clamped both of his hands together in the namaste salutation. Dr. Altbaum wasn't aware that I was standing there. He was busy looking into Nima's ear with an otoscope. Nima flinched when the cold instrument pressed inside his ear. But the doctor relaxed Nima by telling him that he was just looking for the *yeti,* the legendary Abominable Snowman. It was the first time since the Himalayas that I saw Nima laugh.

From the casual way Dr. Altbaum was acting, I was starting to think that maybe Nima wasn't seriously ill. Perhaps the doctor would merely suggest a good strong dose of vitamins, combined with healthy meals and lots of rest.

Finally Dr. Altbaum told me to come inside the examining room. The first thing he wanted to know was how much weight I thought Nima had lost in the past six months. I told him about twenty to twenty-five pounds. He then wanted to know if I had ever seen Nima spit up blood. I said I hadn't, but John was almost certain he had. As Dr. Altbaum began scribbling in a note pad, I thought back to the day when our worst suspicions had been confirmed.

We had been laboriously puffing up a particularly steep stretch of the trail, when we stopped for a moment to catch our breath. I looked up and saw Nima standing just above. He was breathing heavily, too, but it didn't stop him from helping.

When we reached a rest stop, I leaned back against a rock outcrop next to Nima. I noticed how thin his wrists were. That he had been able to carry so much weight up Everest seemed a miracle. He was coughing again, though not quite as much as earlier.

"You have a bad cold, Nima?" I asked.

"Bad," he said. "Very bad."

"How long have you had it?" I asked.

"Many long times. Many long."

"Have you been to a doctor?"

"Yes," he said. "Nima go spirit doctor of Khumjung. Nima go foreign doctor in Kathmandu. Both doctor good man."

"And what did they say?"

"Nima have TB. But get betters. Much betters."

"You're sure?"

"Yes, betters."

"Do you do what they tell you to do?"

"Spirit doctor say Nima do many prays. Foreign doctor say Nima take many medicines."

"Do you take the medicine?" I asked.

"Some time no able. Up in mountain. No medicines. Some time forget. Medicines are many, many rupees." But then he quickly added, "Nima do many prays."

"You have some medicine with you now?"

"This time Nima forgets to bring."

"When you get back to Kathmandu, you promise to get some more?"

"Yes, Memsahib, Nima promise."

The moment Dr. Altbaum stopped scribbling, a smile came over his face.

"Nima," he said, shoving the note pad into his coat pocket, "tell me something about the Sherpas."

Nima immediately zeroed in one particular Sherpa. His name was Mingma. He was the *sirdar,* or senior Sherpa guide, on our trek. He was one step below Lhakpa, the top Sherpa boss. On more than one occasion John and I both sensed Mingma's subtle but apparent Napoleonic qualities. We liked him, but we were scared to death of stepping out of line. I did, however, feel sorry for Nima. It seemed as if Mingma unnecessarily threw his weight around when it came to Nima. One time, I asked Mingma as diplomatically as possible why he always had to send Nima to lug the firewood, water, or whatever else was needed to set up camp. The look Mingma gave me made me wish I had said nothing.

Now Nima began telling Dr. Altbaum a bit of juicy gossip about Mingma. He said that Mingma had never been to a foreign doctor. He was scared of them. Mingma had only been to Spirit A-Tutu. And one time boss Lhakpa had told Mingma he should go see a foreign doctor in Kathmandu for his bad stomach. But Mingma never went. Mingma claimed that his stomach pains were directly related to his uncle's death. Mingma and his uncle had gotten into an argument over whose turn it was to supply the *chang* (Sherpa beer) for a cousin's wedding. Mingma claimed he was always getting stuck and he called his uncle a "cheap Tamang," the Tamangs being one of the lowland tribes that Sherpas feel superior to. Shortly afterward his uncle died. It was several days later that Mingma began getting stomach pains. Mingma, convinced that his uncle was taking revenge, refused to see anyone but A-Tutu, who could exorcise his uncle's spirit. Nima told Dr. Altbaum and me that he thought Mingma might have just made that whole story up because he didn't want to tell big boss Lhakpa that he was afraid of foreign doctors.

I'm not at all sure that Dr. Altbaum understood anything Nima had been telling him, but he nodded his head, as if to say that it all made perfect sense to him. After about twenty minutes of chatting, Dr. Altbaum helped Nima down from the table and told him to put on his shirt and shoes and join us in the hall when he was finished.

As we left Nima, I felt optimistic and confident. But once outside the examining room, Dr. Altbaum's smile disappeared. His eyes were intense. His voice was firm.

"Elizabeth," he said, "I'm admitting Nima to Norwalk Hospital immediately."

The word *immediately* sent a rush of blood to my head. I felt dizzy and confused. Just seconds earlier Dr. Altbaum was joking around with Nima as if nothing were wrong.

"Is it that serious?" I asked. "I mean, he'll be okay, won't he?" Before I finished saying those words I read the answer on Dr. Altbaum's face.

"Nima," he said, "is gravely ill."

# TWO

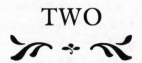

SEEING NIMA AGAIN brought back a flood of memories about our trek. Our motivation for making such a strenuous trip was to explore the rich legends, myths, and realities of the Himalayas for a book John intended to write.

This type of story was not at all typical of John's past books. In recent years he had covered some pretty depressing subjects. One year he stalked a killer virus through Africa. Next, he spent a year investigating a cover-up of a near-meltdown at a nuclear power plant in the United States. Following that, there was a chemical explosion in Italy where I got the dubious honor of helping him do research in the dioxin-ridden area of northern Italy. Two years later, with me as researcher, John had completed two more books. One concerned the crash of a jetliner; the other, the crackup of an airship back in the 1920s.

It was immediately following these two crash stories that John and I came down with a syndrome I called Disaster Overload. The only cure would be a change of scenery. It was now time for us to get out of the depths of disease and sudden death into something uplifting. I thought: What could be more uplifting than the ceiling of the world—where it is said that wisdom and serenity prevail? At least that is what John and I kept telling each other in an effort to convince ourselves that we were doing the right thing.

When we first told our friends our plans they were shocked. Then they were quick to remind us that we were probably the only two in Fairfield County who didn't jog, play tennis, or even take an occasional aerobics class. They were sure we were doomed. And we hadn't even told them about the 175 miles we would face, or the 36,000 feet up and about the same distance down a steep rollercoasterlike profile. Nor did they know about the shaky bamboo bridges and six-inch-wide ledges. We did, however, tell them that we would be spending forty nights in a six-by-eight geodesic tent that often would be pitched in snow and ice.

When we told our accountant of these plans, he wasn't nearly as subtle as our friends. "Are you two dead from the neck up?" he asked. We reassured him that by the time we were ready to leave we would be in great physical shape. But we soon learned that he wasn't as concerned for our physical well-being as he was for our profit-and-loss statement. "Fuller," he said to John, "you're a writer. Writers can't take one quarter of the fiscal year chasing the Abominable Snowman."

I told him how necessary it was for us to do something positive and upbeat. We were becoming too bogged down in the material world. Besides, we felt that Western civilization might just be ready for some Eastern wisdom. He barely responded as I began to outline our objective for exploring Eastern mysticism, the peaceful monks and lamas in the Buddhist monasteries, the genteel Sherpa people, the yeti stories, the mysterious Shangri-la called Shambala alleged to be hidden deep in the Himalayas. And he drew a complete blank when I added one other objective. It would be a whimsical postscript based on an ancient Madison Avenue joke with metaphysical overtones.

In the joke, a successful advertising man learns that there is a lama high in the Himalayas who is supposed to be the only one in the world who knows the meaning of Truth. Fed up with Madison Avenue, the ad man sells his agency, his house in Scarsdale, his Brooks Brothers suits, travels to Tibet and then climbs to the highest monastery. There he asks the lama whom he has struggled all this distance to reach, "What is the meaning of Truth?" The lama simply says, "My good pilgrim, Truth is a fountain."

The man is furious. "You mean to tell me I sold my ad agency, my house, my clothes, and my Mercedes SL-450 just to hear that Truth is a fountain?"

The lama looks puzzled and hurt. "You mean it *isn't?*"

By the time we had finished telling the joke, our accountant had tucked his ledger under his arm and gone out the door, muttering to himself.

The day we boarded Pan Am 1 to begin our forty-day Himalayan research trip, we were physically prepared—thanks to a rigorous six-month training program of daily hiking around the hills of Connecticut. On top of that, we both had had complete medical checkups. John had even gone for a stress test. During the six months it took to prepare for the trip, I actually managed to convince myself that I was going to enjoy trekking eight hours each day, sleeping in a tent, and bathing in ice-cold rivers. But as the plane took off, there were the nagging doubts and anxieties over leaving behind Western comforts, especially my blow dryer, Mr. Coffee, and a nightly glass or two of wine.

Once we arrived in Kathmandu, our expedition outfitters at Mountain Travel left nothing to chance. We were a little surprised and felt slightly self-indulgent when we learned that the two of us would require three Sherpas—Mingma, Pasang, and Nima—and ten porters from the lowlands to carry the gear and food along a trail that was so rugged no horse or donkey could negotiate it. Yaks could be had only after we reached some twelve thousand feet.

Most important was the list of dos and don'ts spelled out for us by Bobby Chettri at the Mountain Travel headquarters before we set out. Chettri, a young Nepalese who spoke perfect English, was responsible for making all of our final arrangements for the expedition.

"You'll notice," Chettri said, "that whenever the Sherpas give you something, or receive something from you, they use both hands. This is a mark of respect. When you make an offering to a deity, use both hands. The hearth, the fireplace in a house, is very sacred. You—as foreigners—are polluted. Yes, polluted. But if you're invited into a house, by all means go in. Protocol demands that you take off your shoes. Follow your host inside the house. Don't sit down until he suggests it. You might accidentally sit somewhere sacred."

There were so many details in Chettri's guidelines that it seemed impossible to remember them all. He instructed us on the conventional greeting, with folded palms in front of the face and the word *namaste,* and he implored us not to succumb to the children who asked for *mettai,* or candy. "Please," Chettri added, "we don't want Nepal to turn into a nation of beggars."

When we got onto the subject of mountain sickness, John and I both began to feel lightheaded. Since it could be such a dangerous condition, with death a distinct possibility, I was worried about how to tell the difference between my sure-to-be-imagined symptoms and the real ones.

Chettri continued, "Please remember the procedure on emergencies. Helicopter evacuation is very expensive, plus unreliable. It may be five or six days before you get a helicopter, if you're lucky. Even if you can get yourself carried by a Sherpa or a yak to a STOL [short takeoff and landing] airstrip, you never know when a plane can get in. So be careful."

With that, he handed us instructions that covered some twenty single-spaced, legal-size pieces of paper, with information on footgear, clothing, medical emergencies, trekking permits, daily routine on the trail, and protocol.

John and I bowed namaste to Bobby Chettri and headed out across the Durbar Marg, the wide main street in Kathmandu, carefully dodging cars, bicycles, and rickshaws. We intentionally avoided the charm and allure of the old city of Kathmandu and went straight for the luxury of the modern Soaltee Oberoi, across the city from the Biman Airport on the Kalimati Road, and out of the noise of the inner city. We had picked the hotel because we knew it was to be our last touch of civilization before we set off on our journey.

The following morning we were picked up at 6:30 in front of the hotel and driven three hours out of Kathmandu by Land Rover. We were squeezed into a small back seat smothered by the packs and equipment. There was a driver, Mingma, and Nima in the front seat. Pasang had gone ahead to organize the porters at Dolaghat, two hours away.

Nima, meeting us for the first time, smiled at us, half shy, half bold, covering his mouth as he coughed. Because the gear was so tightly packed around us, Nima jumped out and attempted to make more room for us.

"Sorry not much room," he said. "Short ride."

Nima adjusted one of the largest heads of cabbage I had ever seen, moving it from under our feet.

"If Memsahib get too little room, I carry in front seat," Nima said. Then he jumped back in the front seat, and the Land Rover lurched ahead.

It was a chilly morning. We were glad we had kept our parkas out. We burrowed down in them and watched the nearly empty streets of Kathmandu flash by in the gray light of early morning. Before long, we were rising slowly along what is called the Chinese Road, which leads to the Tibetan border, some seventy miles to the north. It is a snaking, twisting road, with horseshoe curves. We were fighting a losing battle with the gear, which kept spilling over from the rear compartment into our sitting space. John kept struggling with two straw stools and the enormous cabbage at the side of his knee, which simply would not stay in place. Nima finally reached back and put it on his lap. "I keep," he said. But he had less room than we.

The Land Rover bumped through the village of Banepa, where the porters of the old, classic Everest expeditions used to gather on a wide plain for the assignment of their seventy-pound basket loads. They would use hundreds of porters to support a fifteen- or twenty-man climbing team.

The rise to the rim of the Kathmandu Valley unrolled captivating scenery. In the distance, tiny toylike houses with musty, earth-colored walls and roofs that looked like straw hats blended into the lush green amphitheater of terraces. Passing through the village, we saw Nepalese women walk along the road, ignoring the drivers' frantic horn blasts. They carried enormous loads of firewood on their backs. Indifferent to their struggles, an elderly man sat in front of his ornate, carved doorway smoking a hookah water pipe as small children scrambled near him. An early-morning marriage procession marched by, led by a noisy, squeaky band. Behind them, a young boy was carrying his two-year-old sister on his back, laughing as he bounced her up and down. More women paraded along the road, their shawls pulled tightly about them to fight off the morning cold.

As the Land Rover bumped on, we headed straight into the morning sun, moving down into the Indravati Valley.

Suddenly, near the village of Dhuklikhel, the dramatic jagged fence of the great white Himalayas sprung into full view. We had only been teased by their peaks driving up from the Kathmandu plains. Now they struck with all their force. Although the snow-blanketed peaks marked the border of Tibet, they looked close enough to touch. The mist shrouding the valleys of the nearby mountains made the great sawtooth range seem as if it were half-floating in the distance.

Soon the view was lost again as the Land Rover moved down deeper into a new valley. There was a sheer drop on our left, with an occasional cave-in along the road. Close to us, the vegetation seemed almost tropical, in spite of the morning frost.

Finally, we pulled into Dolaghat, the last village you can reach by car. From there on the roads disappear and the trail to Everest consists of beaten footpaths and slippery rock ledges that go in only two directions—straight up and straight down. For most expeditions, Dolaghat marks the beginning of the approach march toward Everest.

The scene in Dolaghat was confused. A crowd was standing about on the road, staring at our gear as it was unloaded under Mingma's supervision. This was the first time we had seen him in action. Even before John and I climbed down, Mingma was shouting orders and snapping everyone to attention, including John and me. But I was glad of that. An expedition of fifteen people—porters, Sherpa guides, and us—needed an authority figure.

Included in Mingma's orders was the assignment of Nima as our constant companion and guide. Mingma and Pasang would have to move ahead of us by at least an hour so they could stake out our campsite for lunch, dinner, and for overnight. What none of us knew at the time Mingma gave those orders was just how much of a companion Nima would become. Who could have predicted, as we headed out of the village that very first day, that I would come down with mountain sickness halfway through the trek? Or that Nima would run two hours in blizzard conditions to bring the spirit doctor of Khumjung to my rescue? Or all the times Nima would have to tie a rope around my waist and follow me down steep mountain passes? Nima would say, "Memsahib knee same like chicken," referring to a rare condition called "sahib's knee," where the knee buckles going downhill.

But there were the good times too. Almost every evening Nima, John, and I would sit around the campfire exchanging stories. Nima would tell us eerie tales of how the Yeti had been known to ravage entire villages. Or we would hear chilling accounts of how he escaped near-death on various expeditions.

In turn, John and I would tell Nima all about Cape Canaveral, the Empire State Building, and television. Nima didn't seem to find it hard to believe that rockets are regularly shot into space, or that there were buildings with a hundred or more floors, and elevators that could take you up in a matter of seconds. He did, however, find it almost impossible to believe that there were entire stores that sold nothing but American blue jeans.

That was how our trek began. That was how we began to know and love Nima. But back in Connecticut, as we prepared to take Nima to the hospital the day after his visit to Dr. Altbaum, the long trek in the Himalayas seemed like a vague, half-remembered dream, except perhaps for the time we said good-bye to Nima in the mountains. That scene still stood out vividly.

It was on the morning of the last day of our trek. A hand siren suddenly screeched as we sat by the Lukla airstrip. I looked up and saw a plane weaving precariously toward us. As it floated down, its cardboardlike wings wobbled in the treacherous air currents. Finally it leveled off, skimmed over the edge of the cliff, and bumped down in a cloud of dust, scattering stones everywhere.

Nima was nowhere to be seen. He had simply cleaned up the campsite and disappeared. We were worried. The plane would be taking off almost immediately, while the weather was still good and the wind had died down, a rare occasion. I looked back toward the campsite and saw a slim figure running toward the plane. As Nima came up beside us, we could hear that his breathing was painfully labored. He was carrying two exquisitely molded garlands of rhododendrons. They were held together by string and sprinkled with water to keep them fresh. He put them around our necks tenderly and said namaste with tears in his eyes. John and I were so moved that we had to turn away not to show our own tears.

We moved toward the plane and suddenly realized that we had made no plans to help Nima with his medical problem. He was standing there, waving good-bye, looking frailer and thinner than when our trek had begun. As we waited for the door of the plane to open, John said, "We didn't even ask him if he'd consider coming to the States, where he might get better medical help."

"I'll find out," I said. "Wait here."

I rushed over to Nima. "Would you like to come and visit us?" I asked.

He looked surprised. "To come to you country?"

"Yes," I said.

"Yes. Someday Nima come say 'Namaste to Memsahib and Sahib.'"

"No, not *someday*, Nima. John and I mean very, very soon."

*John and Nima pause along the trail from Dholaghat to Tengboche.*

"Nima no money," he said.

"We will send you a ticket."

He nodded his head. "Nima like go visits Memsahib, Sahib."

"You're sure?" I asked.

"Nima sure."

"Good. We will talk to your boss when we get to Kathmandu. When you get there, you talk to him about it."

John was calling to me. The door of the plane was open and other trekkers were getting on. I rushed over to John and together we were swept into the plane's cabin. It would take half a year for Nima to arrive in America—and with Dr. Altbaum's diagnosis, it was none too soon.

# THREE

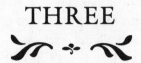

THE EVENING BEFORE we took Nima to the hospital, Dr.
Altbaum phoned. He told us that Nima would be undergo-
ing two difficult and painful tests. One was a broncoscopy,
during which a probe would be forced through his nose to
one lung and extract some tissue. It sounded terrifying. But
no worse than the bone-marrow drill they would also do.
This involved boring directly into the spinal column, with
at least ten seconds of excruciating pain. Because of Nima's
frail condition, no anesthetic could be given.

On the drive down the Connecticut Thruway, we tried to
reassure and warn Nima at the same time. It was not easy.
We did not want him to face two harrowing ordeals without warning. But at the same time, we had to impress upon
him that all of this was extremely important if he was to get
well.

In a way, we underestimated Nima. He seemed to know
instinctively how sick he was. We told him that some of the
tests would be uncomfortable, and he nodded and smiled
from the back seat.

"American doctors very good," he said, as if trying to
convince himself. "Sahib and Memsahib be at hospital with
Nima?"

Nima seemed more worried about being separated from

us than he did about the tests. We reassured him that we would be either at the hospital or within easy reach. He seemed pleased with that. Then he half mumbled to himself, "Nima very brave. Nima no scared chicken."

We went up with him to his room. In minutes he was in his pajamas and robe, lying back on the white sheets and pillows, looking as if he were at Club Med for a well-needed rest. It wasn't long before a parade of doctors began filing in, some involved with the broncoscopy and bone-marrow drill, others to get their first glimpse of a Sherpa.

We had brought several illustrated books on Everest and the Himalayas to keep Nima from getting homesick, and to divert his attention from what was going to happen to him. He inevitably invited every doctor and nurse who set foot into his room to see on the book's photos how far he had climbed up Everest, and to show them the tiny village at the base of the high mountain where he had been born and raised. Then he would carefully pull out the beat-up Polaroid of his family. He made certain that everyone could see how old his mother was and that they understood that she was the bravest woman in all of Phakding.

There would be no major testing that first day in the hospital. Nima would simply undergo some routine blood and urine tests. It would give him a chance to get used to the hospital, and from every indication it seemed that the staff would make him feel at home and comfortable. In fact, Nima appeared more reassured than John or I. But that would be only temporary. After his first blood test, Nima had a change of heart.

"Memsahib, Sahib, Nima say many thank you for help get betters." He no longer looked as if he were at a resort hotel. He was sitting up perfectly rigid in the hospital bed. There was a nurse standing at his side. She was flipping through one of the books as she waited for Nima to unlock his folded arms so she could draw more blood.

I noticed that he looked even paler than when he was helped off the Air India plane nearly forty-eight hours earlier. "John and I know that very soon you will be healthy again."

"Namaste," Nima said without unlocking his folded arms.

"Nima," John said, "the nurse is waiting for you to give her your arm so she can do another blood test."

But Nima was not about to unlock his arms. In fact, he seemed to clutch them even tighter.

"Memsahib," he said, "I think Nima go see holy lama in you village before good, strong nurse get more bloods."

With those words, the heavyset nurse widened her eyes, adjusted her glasses, and left the room mumbling something about a shift change.

"Nima," John said, "that's impossible. We have no lamas in Fairfield County."

Nima looked from John to me as if we were putting him on. He was convinced that our villages, as his, were crawling with monks and lamas, and had no shortage of monasteries. I confirmed what John said. Nima then looked at both of us as if we were some kind of heathens.

The Sherpas' religion—Buddhism is totally fused with their everyday life. No Sherpa would ever dream of going on a dangerous expedition—or to a hospital—without first getting a lama's seal of approval. In fact, before Nima came to America he went to his village lama for the go-ahead. Then there was Pasang, the second Sherpa in command on our trek. Pasang had reluctantly joined our amateurish venture after the lama at Tengboche Monastery told him that the dangerous Everest expedition he was scheduled for would not be propitious. Pasang reported this news back to boss Lhakpa, and Lhakpa put him on our trek.

While John went out of the room for a cigarette, I began trying to explain to Nima that most Americans *do* believe in God, but instead of lamas we have priests, rabbis, and ministers. And instead of temples we have churches, although on second thought I realized we do have temples but they're Jewish temples, not Buddhist. Finally, Nima said that he would like to go to a Jewish temple and see a rabbi. I told him I would take him to a temple, but not until he got out of the hospital. Then I said I would see if a rabbi would be visiting the hospital and, if so, would ask him to come by and see Nima.

When one of the nurses on the new shift came into the room, I asked about the rabbi. She said that she couldn't be certain if there would be one around. She was positive, however, that a Catholic priest would be making rounds after visiting hours. Nima settled on the priest.

I hated to leave Nima alone to face the series of tests, but we had no choice. The head nurse had finally suggested that perhaps the staff could get more cooperation from Nima if we were not around. We hugged Nima good-bye, all the while reminding him that if he felt as if he *really* needed us at any time of the day or night we would come back.

The moment we stepped through our front door, the phone rang. It was Nima.

"Daily best wishes, Memsahib."

"Nima," I said, "are you okay?"

"Nima many okays."

After several seconds of silence, he told me why he was calling.

"Nurse say, 'Nima eat you dinners.' Nima say, 'Nima no eat dead chicken meats.' Other nurse, doctor, say same things."

We had forgotten to tell the staff that Nima was a strict vegetarian—although not all Sherpas are. Technically, it is against the Buddhist religion for a Sherpa to kill an animal. But there are loopholes. Nima once told us that Sherpas are allowed to eat meat—provided they do not personally kill the animal. Usually they find a Hindu who, for a stipend, will willingly wipe out chickens, goats, yaks and sheep.

I asked Nima to put on the nurse who had dialed the call. She said that Nima just kept repeating that he couldn't eat dead chicken meat. The nurse assumed he meant that the broiled chicken hadn't been properly prepared so she cut it up to prove that it was not raw. After we informed her of the situation, the nurse said she would see to it that Nima was sent up a cheese omelet and french fries.

Before we hung up, she reassured us that Nima was just fine. He seemed to be proud of the fact that he was not afraid of American doctors, she said. In fact, he had been telling her all about a friend of his who was scared of any doctor except the spirit doctors back in the Himalayas. I was sure Nima was talking about his friend Mingma, whom I didn't really blame for being afraid of any doctor outside his own hometown.

I had run into the reverse situation myself while we were on the home ground of Nima and Mingma six months before. I was unexpectantly stricken with altitude, or mountain, sickness just about as far away from medical assistance as you can get. John and I had taken precautions to avoid getting this dreaded syndrome by making a conscious effort to acclimatize slowly. But in spite of our efforts, all the symptoms crept up on me at twelve thousand feet.

Our Sherpas were trained to recognize the warning signals: loss of appetite, dizziness, weakness, nausea, difficulty in breathing, and Cheyne-Stokes syndrome, which turns you blue and makes you gulp for air. In fact, it was Nima who first noticed that my walking had become unsteady, almost as if I had been drinking. I felt a little light-headed, but I wasn't aware of my clumsiness. I insisted to Nima that I was just tired. We continued onward and upward the rest of the day. By the time we made camp at a village called Namche Bazaar, I was so nauseated and weak that I went to bed without dinner.

The next morning I wasn't feeling any better, but I wasn't any worse either. John, noticing I was not myself, insisted that we descend at least a thousand feet, but I refused to give in. Instead, we climbed through a stinging wind-whipped snowstorm to a rocky bivouac site within an hour's trek of a village called Khumjung. It was there, at thirteen thousand feet, that the symptoms worsened. Breathing was a great effort. I could no longer walk a straight line. Without even consulting me, Mingma rigged up one of our yaks in preparation to haul me down two thousand feet fast. The only cure for mountain sickness is immediate descent, and at least that much of a drop.

I explained to John and our Sherpas that I really appreciated their concern, but I didn't have mountain sickness. I was just very tired. There was no way anyone was going to load me onto the back of a yak. They assured me that I had no choice. If I didn't heed the warning signals, I could die. Nima began relating stories about foreigners who had died along the trail. "Many, many peoples deads," he said somberly. John kept reminding me of what Bobby Chettri had told us: six trekkers in the last year had died of mountain sickness.

But I was not convinced enough to get on the back of that yak, as gentle as Nima claimed he was. Besides, it was already getting dark and starting to snow harder than ever.

The spindrift literally bit into our faces. All I wanted to do was climb into my sleeping bag.

John and our Sherpas were annoyed at my adamant refusal to descend. However, in view of the snowstorm that had suddenly escalated to near-blizzard conditions, they stopped arguing. I think they felt, as I did, that it was risky, even for a sure-footed yak and Sherpas, to descend to the required level. We would have had to squeeze along the side of a precipice on any icy, inches-wide ledge, blinded by the snow, with a three-thousand-foot drop on our right.

By the time we finished dinner, it was snowing and the winds were almost gale force. I was so fuzzy from the events of the day that I don't even remember sliding into my sleeping bag. But I do remember the next thing that happened. Somewhere between ten and twelve o'clock that same night, there was a sound at the flap of our tent. It was Mingma.

"Mrs. Lizzy, the doctor is here," he said. "Nima go Khumjung bring doctor."

My first thought was that I was dreaming. No one could have gone to Khumjung, an hour away, in a blinding storm to bring a doctor back. Then John gently shook me and confirmed what I thought I had heard. We figured that the New Zealand doctor, who was stationed in the village of Khumjung, must have returned unexpectedly from Lukla.

We fumbled around our tent, and fished out a flashlight, boots, and our heavy parkas. Even the slightest movement was an effort. I felt as if I were moving in slow motion. John unzipped the flap of the tent. A thick layer of accumulated snow blew in and whipped across our faces. We yanked up the hoods on our parkas, covering as much of our faces as possible, then ventured out into the storm.

Mingma was waiting for us. When I saw the expression

on his face I really felt rotten. There he was, standing patiently in the raw snowstorm, genuinely concerned about my health. And there I was, only hours earlier, bad-mouthing him to John because he was so officious.

We followed him with our chins tucked downward to fight off the blast of snow. Standing around a blazing fire outside the mess tent were Sherpas I had never seen before. I thought at first that they had come to see the New Zealand doctor. But we later learned they had just come to join in the festivities that would follow.

Inside the mess tent, the only light came from the glow of the campfire. I could discern a figure sitting in the center facing a low table. His craggy face was fixed into permanent grooves and valleys. He was wearing Tibetan garb that looked like heavy layers of sackcloth piled one on top of the other. He was intently rolling small cones of clarified yak butter and placing each cone along the rim of a copper bowl. I glanced around the tent. There was no one who looked even vaguely like a New Zealand doctor.

Mingma introduced us to A-Tutu, the spirit doctor and shaman of Khumjung. The first thing that crossed my mind was that Mingma was getting even with me for telling him to go easier on Nima. The second thing was this was for real. I was about to have some sort of spirit doctor do whatever to me, and there was obviously nothing I could do about it. Nima had gone to a lot of trouble to bring Spirit A-Tutu down from Khumjung.

After the introduction, Mingma threw a blanket down on the dirt floor and told John and me to sit on it next to the spirit doctor. I can't ever remember feeling so cold and yet so hot at the same time. My head throbbed. My entire body ached. I had no idea how I was going to get through this ritual, but I knew that I would have to be gracious and stick it out.

We must have been sitting next to Spirit A-Tutu for close to an hour. I thought he would never stop rolling the butter cones. After all seven of the copper bowls were rimmed with little, soggy cones, he lined them up on the altar, which was on his right. Then he began rolling more butter, but this time placing the cones around the edges of two brass mirrors. Then the mirrors joined the bowls on the altar.

The altar was a crude, makeshift plank covered in a once-white cloth. It sloped dangerously forward. Every time A-Tutu moved I worried that the cups and mirrors would tumble to the tent floor. And worse, he would have to start rolling cones again. When everything was arranged on the altar just the way he wanted it, he began pulling corn and rice out of sacks and spilling it into bowls until they overflowed.

One hour had elapsed since Mingma had deposited us on the blanket. I wasn't sure if I was numb because of the wind and snow blowing into the tent, or if this was just the first sign of death setting in. John had his arm around me, and he was whispering to me what Nima was whispering to him about what was happening.

The next thing that happened was Mingma's mother-in-law appeared at the entrance of the tent. In her arms was a large pan of juniper twigs mixed in with pieces of smoldering branches. She began eagerly blowing the incense around the tent. It didn't take long for the tent to fill up with smoke, and we soon began coughing. Then she placed the pan alongside Spirit A-Tutu, and she sat cross-legged in front on him, grabbing the best seat in the house.

A Tibetan I had never seen before came into the tent and sat next to me. Nima said that he was a friend of Spirit A-Tutu who offered to come down and help carry the doctor's paraphernalia. Pasang was outside preparing the chang for the festivities that would follow. There were also a lot of strays standing around the outside of the tent, occasionally peering in.

Mingma motioned for Nima to go outside. Nima sprang to his feet and picked his way through the cramped tent. Seconds later, he returned carrying what looked like a drum on loan from Macy's Thanksgiving Day Parade. Nima seemed to know exactly what to do. He knelt down between Spirit A-Tutu and John, propped the drum upright on its long, rough-hewn pole, and grasped it with both hands.

Then there was silence. A-Tutu sat up straight. He took the mirror from the altar and held it up, as if he were looking into it. With his other hand, he picked up a piece of cloth the size of a dish towel. Then in a low, deep voice he began to chant. As he did so, he placed the mirror back on the altar and sprinkled rice on it. Nima whispered to John that A-Tutu was supposed to be calling in the spirits and inviting them to speak through him.

After about fifteen minutes of chanting, the still body of Spirit A-Tutu began to tremble. His breathing got heavy and he began making guttural noises. He picked up an enormous headdress and put it on. Then he took a large bundle of what looked like rags—hundreds of tiny swatches of material, all colors and shapes, tied together—and covered his face with it. With his free hand, he began pounding the drum, keeping rhythm with his chanting.

I looked over at Nima to see how he was taking all of this. When he caught my eye, he grinned. Seeing Nima grin made me feel more comfortable. I don't know why. It probably had something to do with my own irreverence.

A-Tutu's body moved from a slight tremble to a heavy, shuddering tremor. His voice changed to a high-pitched singing, which he alternated with a hissing and a blowing through his nose. Although there seemed to be a lot going on, he somehow maintained a hypnotic beat. In fact, his beat was so hypnotic that the man sitting on my left, the Tibetan, began quivering just like A-Tutu. Mingma and Pasang scrambled over to where he was sitting and dragged him out of the tent. Once outside, Mingma slapped him in the face and Pasang lobbed chang on him. I thought that all this was part of the ceremony, and that I would be next. But Nima whispered to John that it simply was bad luck for two people to go into a trance at the same time.

The ritual continued as if nothing had happened. Mingma's mother-in-law, who was sitting directly in front of A-Tutu, took a small piece of cloth that she had been wearing and tied it onto A-Tutu's bundle. Then she began tossing rice into his hand. According to Nima, the evil spirits were now supposed to be visible in the brass mirror that A-Tutu was holding. Mingma gave Nima the cue to have John present a coin as an offering. Mingma then reached over, took the coin from John's hand, and placed it on the altar. The offering was supposed to be to Shrindi, a spirit who was requested to enter A-Tutu's body.

After the coin was placed on the altar, A-Tutu began to shake even more violently. With that, Mingma's mother-in-law began asking questions. The idea behind the questions was that, when A-Tutu was in a trance state, the gods and spirits would speak through him and tell him what was wrong with me. For thirty minutes Mingma's mother-in-law continued to ask questions. Each time she tossed a handful of rice, she crouched forward with a glazed-over eyes and waited excitedly for his chanted answer.

I thought it was a little strange that she was asking so many questions about my health. She didn't even know me. Later, my suspicions were confirmed. Nima told us that Mingma's mother-in-law had only asked once what was wrong with me. From there, she shifted into next year's trade with Tibet, focusing on the rate of salt-grain exchange and the price of Tibetan wool. The questions soon degenerated into pure gossip about her neighbors in Khumjung, their husbands, the other woman, the other man. She was the only person I've ever met who talked more than Mingma. If I hadn't been so sick, I would not have minded her milking poor Spirit A-Tutu on my time.

Finally the questions stopped. A-Tutu began making sounds similar to that of a caged bird. His shaking, which had slowed down during the questions, now intensified. Mingma crawled over to me, signaled his mother-in-law to give up her seat, and slid me over to where she had been sitting. The second I sat down, Spirit A-Tutu grabbed my hand and began licking it. After that, he vomited. Mingma, who had been squatting next to me, told me to get on all fours. I did. Before I even had a chance to worry about what was going to happen next, A-Tutu picked up his large bundle of rags and clubbed me three times, sending a plume of dust everywhere. That wrapped up the ceremony. Spirit A-Tutu matter-of-factly packed up his rags and headdress, dismantled the altar, and went outside to join the others in a cup of chang.

As we walked back to our tent, Nima told us that the spirits, speaking through A-Tutu, diagnosed my illness as mountain sickness. The prognosis was positive: I would be cured after descending two thousand feet. The next morning we did as the spirits ordered.

After four days, I was as good as new. And John and I were ready to give the Everest base camp another shot.

Now, in Connecticut, Nima was facing the reverse mysteries of Western medicine, and he was as unprepared for that as I had been for the pounding of the spirit drum. But when we arrived at the hospital to visit Nima on his second day there, he was almost back to his old self—at least he had some color back in his face. I don't know if it was the priest's visit, the good night's rest, or the attractive blond nurse at his side flipping through one of his books.

"Namaste, Nima," we said as we entered his room.

"Namaste, Memsahib, Sahib." Then he added as cheerfully as I've ever heard him, "Good day!"

We weren't in the room for more than a few seconds when Nima reached over to the table and showed us two holy cards and a pair of rosary beads given to him by the priest. Nima called the beads "*mani* stones." Rubbing the rosary beads between his index finger and thumb, he told us that he had woken up in the middle of the night and became scared all over again about being in the hospital. He got out of bed and went into the hall to find a doctor or nurse to dial our number. But when he finally found a nurse she said that it was too late to phone us. She wheeled him back to his room in a "quick chair" and helped him into bed. He still couldn't sleep, so he picked up the "mani stones" and began praying—and that was when he fell back to sleep. The next morning, he woke up still clutching the "mani stones." He was no longer afraid.

Over the following two days Nima underwent the broncoscopy and bone-marrow drill with reasonable calmness and courage, and with the rosary beads firmly implanted in his fist. But until all the tests were completed—some would take days—the doctors could not be certain of just how far the TB had penetrated his system. They were, however, confident that he was not contagious. Still, they insisted on our taking a skin test to see if by any chance we had encountered a contagious strain of the disease on our long trek. Later, we learned that neither we nor Nima had any such problem.

Nima could come back home now, but he would have to follow a strict regimen to regain his health. Most important, he would have to take two courses of rifampin and ethambutol—drugs unavailable in Nepal that were absolutely necessary to take over an eighteen-month period. He would also have to eat a well-balanced diet and concentrate on building his weight. Equally important would be plenty of rest.

The temporary prognosis was good. We drove home from the hospital in considerably higher spirits than when we brought him there.

From the afternoon that Nima got out of the hospital, there was a steady improvement in his health. The first week he weighed in on Dr. Altbaum's scale two pounds heavier, the second five, and by the end of a month he had a total weight gain of nearly fifteen pounds. Along with the weight came strength. Nima constantly told us that if he didn't work he would go crazy. To avoid that possibility, we encouraged him to watch television.

In less than a week after his return from the hospital, Nima had gained enough stamina to lounge around the house and watch everything from "Sunrise Services" straight through to Johnny Carson. John and I were delighted with his newfound interest. Until Nima was well enough to go to night school and to take a first aid course, he could be entertained and at the same time learn about Western civilization. Nima no longer looked at television as just a "good box with good color." He looked at each show with the interest of a potential sponsor. John and I knew that he was absorbing what he was watching because his vocabulary proved it. But what we didn't know was just how television was affecting his view of reality.

# FOUR

DURING THE CHILLY HIMALAYAN EVENINGS around the campfire, we had gradually learned of Nima's roots. Like most of the Sherpas, his ancestors had struggled over the pass at Nangpa La centuries before in search of greener pastures than the bare, browned Tibetan plateau offered. Aided by yaks or *zopkios,* the crossbreed of the yak and oxen, they made their way down past the inhospitable glaciers of the Everest region, where they found fertile soil at unusually high altitudes.

Scrounging a living from potatoes, buckwheat, barley, and leading their yaks to graze at the highest pastures near Everest, the Sherpas had been able to open commerce with Tibet over the pass to obtain salt and wool, and to establish the precarious trade route to Namche Bazaar and below.

From the age of six, Nima was cutting wood in the forest with an ax, hauling loads on his back for many miles, along with daily trips to the river a half-mile away, to carry water. By the time Nima was eight, he began carrying the vegetables grown in their rocky soil to Namche Bazaar for the Saturday market there. He was proud of his strength, and thought nothing of loading a forty-pound basket on his back for the grueling four-hour climb up the mountainside to Namche.

When he was nine, he prepared to go to the Hillary school in Kunde. Not all Sherpa children were as fortunate. Some families needed their children at home to help with the yaks and crops, others lived too far from the school, and still others considered school a luxury that they just couldn't afford. But Nima's parents, although not wealthy, felt they could survive without Nima's hands in the field. Nima told us that his parents sent him to school not only for an education, but for discipline as well. And with good cause.

Once when his father had put him in charge of negotiating a herd of yak—each heftier and more stubborn than a cow—along a trail, seven-year-old Nima and twelve yaks had reached a rickety bridge that stretched across the raging Dudh Khosi River. Nima's attention turned to slinging stones at a chir pine. As one stone after another slammed against the tree, half the herd was being swept away by the current. That evening Nima reluctantly returned to his home minus six yaks. According to Sherpa belief, it is a grave sin to strike a child no matter what the reason. But Nima's father didn't look on losing half the family wealth to the Dudh Khosi as just any reason.

Nima was not spared the firm hand of his father that night, but he was eventually forgiven. Nima, however, never forgot his carelessness.

Nor did he forget how, as a small boy, his mother was constantly visited by other mothers in and around the village. They complained that for little or no reason Nima would haul off and paste their kids. But none of the crying and pleading Nima's mother did could stop him from being such a bully.

I asked Nima what made him eventually stop clipping the other kids. He told us that, finally, his mother got fed up with his behavior and took him to see the high lama at

Tengboche Monastery. At the monastery, the lama told Nima that if he kept pushing around the other kids, he would return as a snake after he died. From that moment on, Nima learned to control his temper.

Sherpas believe true happiness can be gained only after they have learned to live in harmony with their family and fellow villagers. Perhaps that is one reason why the Sherpa people seem to have a zest and joy for life that is lacking in so many people of the Western world. Neither are their lives complicated by a compulsive desire for material acquisition. But Nima did tell us that it is very good for a Sherpa to be rich. The rich Sherpa derives great pleasure from giving away much of his wealth, because he knows that in doing so he gains merit for his next life. According to Nima, when the very rich, generous Sherpa dies, he goes up very high. It is the "poor, cheap Khamba," Nima said, who comes back as a snake.

Although there is no caste system in Nepal, this doesn't mean that prejudices are nonexistent. It is true that Sherpas are devout Buddhists, and the underlying premise of Buddhism is love and compassion for all. But, according to Nima, it is also true that you can have love and compassion for the "no-good tribes" without having them live in your village or marrying your sister.

Two tribes Nima viewed with prejudice were the Tamangs and Khambas. The Tamangs are sandwiched between Kathmandu and the Sherpa country far up in the Solu Khumbu. All of our porters were Tamangs. I once asked Nima why there were so few Tamang guides. Without mincing words he told me, "No Tamang smart enough to be good guide. Only Sherpa make good guide."

When Nima got off on the subject of the Tamangs it was useless to argue with him. He would cite crimes to back up his claim that went back forty years, to a time when some Tamang had ripped off a Sherpa's chicken. But Nima went a little easier on the Khambas, mainly because the Khambas share the exact same descent as the Sherpas, both claiming Tibetan lineage. The only difference is that the Sherpas were in the Solu Khumbu years before the Khambas. Because the Khambas were recent immigrants, arriving in Nepal with few belongings and little money, they had no choice but to do menial labor for the Sherpas. However, unlike the Tamangs, the Khambas were assimilated into Sherpa society. They now own land, houses, yaks, and some few have even married into the old established Sherpa families. But again according to Nima, "A Khamba is still a Khamba."

Nima began school when he was eight years old. Because the school was a full day's climb from his village of Phakding, commuting was impossible. Fortunately, his father had a friend who lived in the same village as the school. The friend invited Nima to live with his family in Kunde, where Sir Edmund Hillary's school was located. Not far away was the local *gomba*, or monastery, which had quite a reputation in the Himalayas—and outside too. It contained one of the two purported yeti skulls known to exist—a fact that was of little interest to Nima. He fully believed that the yeti existed, and even claimed to have heard the eerie yeti cry on several occasions. But he insisted that he didn't have to be shown a strange red skull with tufts of hair protruding from it as proof.

The first day Nima left his home for school, he set out before the sun came up. He put on two shirts, a heavy woven pair of trousers, and a Tibetan wool jacket, for which his mother had traded several sacks of potatoes. He had no shoes to wear, but his tiny feet had been toughened to the point where he could cross rocks, ice, or snow without feeling cold or bruised.

On his back he carried a large inverted conical basket, seen everywhere on the trail. It was suspended by stout cord and a headband across his forehead. In the basket was a gift of rice and potatoes for the family he would be staying with, along with some barley, which would be made into a thick paste known as *tsampa*, a Sherpa and Tibetan staple.

He bowed namaste to his entire family and started along the rocky trail that led toward Namche Bazaar and Khumjung, his bare leathery feet stepping on the more polished rocks, which had been worn down to the luster of mother-of-pearl by the generations of traders that had gone before him. The trail followed along the raging Dudh Khosi for almost two hours until it blended with a blue pine forest at the base of the steep terraced rock stairway that climbed up toward Namche. Along the river, Nima shied away from the giant beehives that sat menacingly inside huge pine trees.

After a taxing three-hour ascent, Nima refreshed himself at a tea stall in Namche, where tiny Sherpa shops lined the rocky paths that formed the illusion of streets in the small village. By the time he climbed the precipitous saddle on the ridge behind the village, there was snow and ice on the ground. On reaching Kunde, it was almost dark. Nima's education was about to begin.

During those four years at the Hillary school, Nima learned arithmetic, how to read and write Sanskrit, and a little English. For entertainment he danced and sang Sherpa folk songs, and played in the shade of the great mountain range; only occasionally did he bop a kid.

By the time Nima was twelve years old, he was ready to leave school and go out into the real world. He was no longer illiterate, and to Nima that meant one thing: he had a good chance of eventually working his way up to the position of Sherpa guide, or later a sirdar.

It was only a year later when a leading Sherpa from the former Hillary expedition dropped by his house for a cup of tea with Nima's family. Although Nima was only fourteen, his ability to climb with heavy loads was widely noted. Asked if he would like to work as a Sherpa guide for Mountain Travel, Nima leaped at the chance, and set off along the undulating trail to Kathmandu with his family's blessing.

After several treks out of Pokhara in the Annapurna region, up along the rugged trails to Jomson and Muktinath, his strength caused him to be singled out for the famous 1975 Chris Bonnington expedition on Everest. He soon impressed the Bonnington staff not only with his carrying strength but his organizational ability. He helped sort out the twenty tons of gear, equipment, and food at the Kathmandu Airport for relay on to a supply base at Kunde, involving over a thousand boxes. Like all Sherpas who would be facing the overwhelming hazards of the Ice Fall—the dangerous cliff of ice at the base of Mount Everest—and Western Cwm, he was delighted with the issue of heavy parkas, boots, gloves, thermal underwear, and other cold-weather gear given to the Sherpas. This was as much of a prize as the high-altitude pay.

As an Ice-Fall porter, carrying up to twenty-two thousand feet, Nima faced one of the most hazardous assignments. With forty-five pounds on his back, he would have to negotiate the huge blocks of ice, many bigger than houses, which could at any minute tumble down the steep frozen waterfall, crushing everyone in its path. In addition, the crevasses shifted unpredictably, leaving unmeasured chasms below them. Many were crossed by fragile alumi-

*Nima along the trail in the Solu-Khumbu. Although his rucksack is light here, he has carried 45 pounds up 24,000 feet in past expeditions.*

num ladders, where one slip would be fatal. The Ice Fall had claimed many lives, and every trip up and down it from the Base Camp increased the hazard mathematically.

Nima made a total of twenty-eight round trips over this steep and threatening glacial mass. The Western Cwm was hardly less hazardous, again with shifting crevasses that at one time almost pitched an entire climbers' camp down into an ice cave. Nima survived ably, and went on to serve on several other treks and expeditions.

Two years later, Nima was a veteran, strong and favored, even though he was still in his teens. He set out with enthusiasm for Darjeeling, en route to the Indian Army expedition to climb Kangchenjunga. It was at this time that he carried higher than twenty-four thousand feet with no oxygen, up and over an ice fall more steep and deadly than Everest's.

Now, one year after that feat, he was sitting in our Weston, Connecticut, home glued to the Sony "color box," as unprepared for this high-tech life-style as John and I would be for scaling Himalayan peaks. But regardless of whether Nima was prepared or not, in less than a month, his ear would become so finely tuned that even when he was in the kitchen with the Cuisinart on, he could recognize his favorite show coming on the air. Since neither John nor I liked to intrude on Nima's privacy, we were not exactly sure what programs commanded his attention. But it quickly became apparent that commercials were his favorites.

The first day Nima felt strong enough to take the bike to our neighborhood shopping center, John and I pointed him in the right direction and then watched him wobble out of sight. He stayed out of sight for four hours.

We were just about to get into the car and go search for

him when our front door was flung open. Nima appeared, looking a little bedraggled and a lot bent over from the weight of his overstuffed backpack, but he was obviously ecstatic about something.

The something turned out to be the goods he had picked up at the grocery store. I had been giving Nima an allowance every time he helped me with small chores around the house. The money, I told him, was his to do with whatever he liked—except I did hint that John and I thought it would be a good idea to save most of it for when he went back to Nepal. From the way Nima nodded, I thought he had agreed too. But from the looks of the jammed backpack I was wrong.

First Nima led us into the living room and told us to sit by the fire. When he was sure that we were comfortable, he began to unload the pack. The first thing out was a large economy-size box of Tide. He presented me with the orange cardboard box as if it were the Hope Diamond. As the box exchanged hands, he told me that it would get even my dirtiest laundry *really, really* white.

I thought I had heard that somewhere before. Then Nima suggested I open the box. Once I did, he had me put out my hand and he gingerly sprinkled some of the granules into my palm. He treated the detergent as if it were gold dust. He asked me how it smelled and I said fantastic. Then I slid my palm under John's nose for his approval. John was more circumspect. He just said yes, and gave me a puzzled look. I wasn't quite sure how long Nima wanted me to admire my gift. He just kept standing there, beaming. Finally, I pointed toward the orange box and told him that it had great color and that I was very excited about getting my clothes really, really white.

Pleased with my reaction, he turned to John with a six-pack of beer. As he passed it to John he said, "It's Miller time"—another phrase familiar to my ear. But it wasn't until Nima went into the kitchen and came back with a couple of glasses and repeated, "It's Miller time," that I made the connection between Nima's gifts and what he had been watching on TV. Everything he spouted was a direct steal from the tube. I was almost afraid to see what else he would pull out of his grab bag, and I had good reason to.

Out came a roll of extra-absorbent Bounty paper towels, complete with demonstration. After Nima unwrapped the roll, he went into the kitchen and brought out the inferior roll I had been using. Then he picked up John's glass of Miller and carefully made two small puddles of beer in the center of the table. Quickly, he soaked up one puddle with Bounty and the other puddle with Brand X, all the while instructing us to watch how Bounty was twice as good as the "no-good towel." Personally, I didn't see any difference.

After the commercial, he took out still another bag. He appeared all set to show us what it was, but then, as if he had suddenly remembered something, he checked his Timex and made a startling breath-sucking gasp. Quickly, he dropped the unopened bag back into his backpack, wiped up the damp table, tore into his room, and turned on "MASH." John and I were left sitting there, too stunned even to speculate on the contents of the bag. But we weren't too stunned to speculate on how anyone could be such a sucker.

Nima's reaction to commercials forced us to face the pure and simple fact that he was as alien to our culture as we were to his. For the previous month, we had taken it for granted that Nima, by osmosis, could adapt to our Western ways with little or no guidance. It was not that we didn't want to take the time to show Nima the ropes. It was more that we didn't want to insult his intelligence. Sherpas are very proud, dignified people.

Now that I think about it, Nima hadn't minded insulting our intelligence when we were in the Himalayas. He didn't for one minute let us out of his sight. Several times I remember becoming very annoyed that Nima always had an eye on us. I spoke to him about it, and he said flatly, "American no smart on mountain. Memsahib and Sahib—if no Sherpa, they deads."

Perhaps Nima did have a valid point. More than once I came close to being planted in the Himalayan soil. But because of Nima's quick reflexes, I'm still above ground.

Of course, I didn't think Nima had to be quite so self-confident about it. I could have reminded him about the time he accidentally took a wrong path and provided John and me with a unintended three-hour scenic tour of the jagged cliffs in and around Junbesi, instead of the thirty-minute tour that Nima's boss, Mingma, and the porters took. When we finally showed up at the campsite, Mingma was on hand to greet us. But it wasn't a greeting I particularly care to remember. In between the Sherpa was the English translation. Mingma told us that when it got dark, he had set Pasang and all the porters to tracking us. He had visions of us floating face down in the Dudh Khosi, or falling off the Lamjura Pass, to say nothing of being attacked by a yeti. Nima was humiliated for having sent us on a three-hour wild goose chase around Junbesi.

The next day, in an attempt to cheer Nima up, John and I related some of the stupid things we had done, and Nima reveled in hearing about these embarrassing moments. Because we were so generous in sharing our humiliations with him, he totally forgot about his. But he didn't forget about ours. And his wild goose chase showed me just how impor-

*Mingma, our senior Sherpa guide* (sirdar), *in a typical pose.*

tant it was for him to always maintain a sense of dignity, especially in front of John and me.

But now, with Nima in our country, it seemed that one incident after another was testing our ability to help Nima adjust to the ways of the modern world, and at the same time, help him to maintain his pride.

In the third week of Nima's recovery John decided it was time to give him a few easy chores. Since we knew that

Nima loved to build fires back in the Himalayas, John let him make the fires in our fireplace. I also decided to familiarize him with the kitchen. Through the air vent in my office I could hear Nima's TV blaring. As soon as a commercial came on, I called through the vent for Nima to turn the electric stove on to preheat and set the dial for 450 degrees, something I had taught him earlier in the day. Then I told him that I would be down in twenty minutes to put the dinner in the oven. Nima seemed anxious to help. Only a second later I heard him coming out of his room. He was still snickering about something on "Gilligan's Island."

Five minutes later, Nima appeared at my office door. "Memsahib," he said, "stove no good." He explained that it was no good because it took a long time to get going. I thought that perhaps he didn't have the dials set correctly. I told him not to worry, and then we both went down to check out the problem.

The dials were set exactly as I had asked. Pleased that Nima had got it right, I reassured him that the stove takes a good ten minutes to really get going. I was just about to walk away when I noticed the faint odor of smoldering paper. At about the same time I saw smoke escaping from inside the oven. I yanked open the oven door and for a brief second thought I was hallucinating. In a neat pile was a meticulously stacked load of firewood, complete with kindling and newspaper. When I realized that my oven was about to melt down to a heap of raw steel, I got hysterical. John, hearing my shrieks tore down the stairs from his office. He took one look at the stoked up electric oven, uttered a few choice words, and began heaving hot water onto the kitchen floor. All the while he was laying into *me*, as if I had anything to do with it.

Finally John calmed down. But he still acted as if *I* had

done it. The entire time Nima had been standing between John and me, almost in a protective manner. From the expression on Nima's face, I could tell he wasn't quite sure what was going on. Nevertheless, since John overtly pointed the blame my way, Nima began eyeing me, as if he too believed it was my fault. But he was also clearly bothered that John had been so angry with me. He began to smooth things over.

"No get mad at Memsahib. Next time Memsahib rest. Nima or Sahib fix stove for dinnertimes."

Nima took me by the arm and led me into his room. He ordered me to sit down and watch the ending of "Gilligan's Island" until dinner was ready.

I couldn't believe it. Nima had almost burned our house down, and he didn't even acknowledge it. His Sherpa pride wouldn't let him.

Finally, John began to give both Nima and me step-by-step instructions on how to use the electric stove. John reminded us every few seconds that you never ever put wood into the oven.

Even more annoying than John's detailed instructions was Nima. Every time John got out a sentence, Nima turned to me and repeated it, making doubly sure I understood.

On one level I sympathized with what John was doing. He did not want Nima to feel as if he alone were totally responsible for the near disaster. Because I'm a big person, I accepted half the blame. Besides, I didn't want Nima to feel uncomfortable in our house. Of course, this time I wished he would have felt just a little less comfortable with the electrical appliances. But this is not to say that we didn't want Nima to feel completely at home with us. It was just that, after three weeks, Nima seemed to be enjoying our way of life without qualification, especially the TV set.

The strange thing was that if Nima hadn't been sick and confined to bed rest for the first month, it probably would have taken him a lot longer to acquaint himself with the Western world. However, because Nima had a constant electronic companion, one that talked to him day and night, he learned about everything—except of course how to use the oven. He even learned about dentures, although it shocked Nima out of his skin the first time he saw the Polident commercial in which a pair of false teeth float around in a glass of water. Nima had never before heard of false teeth. In fact, he had never even been to a dentist. Still, he had teeth as white and straight as a pair of dentures.

It took John and me weeks to realize that this concentrated dose of television could be other than a tool to mildly amuse Nima while he wiled away the hours gaining strength. It never occurred to us when we heard the TV blaring and the sound of Nima's laughter that it was having anything but a therapeutic effect on his health.

The first big clue I got that Nima was taking TV's messages too literally was the time he brought back the Tide, Miller's, and Bounty from the grocery store. More proof came several days later when I discovered what was inside the final mystery package that remained unopened when Nima realized he was late for "MASH."

If I hadn't gone into his bathroom to check for refills on his medicine, I would have been denied the opportunity to see just how seriously commercials could affect the unsuspecting mind. Stacked neatly below his six plastic containers of medicine were three family-size tubes of toothpaste. Each tube was a different brand. Each had been partially squeezed into. My first inclination was not to nose around Nima's personal articles. I know how it used to affect me when John would make unnecessary comments on the various shampoos, creme rinses, and soaps I had lined up in our medicine cabinet. But my sense of curiosity got the better of me.

I went into the kitchen where Nima was whipping up a four-egg cheese omelet with enough french fries to start a fast-food chain. After he turned off the Cuisinart, I asked why he didn't first use one tube, and when that was empty, start another.

The answer I got would have exhilarated half of Madison Avenue. After Nima poured the omelet mixture into the skillet, he went into his bedroom and returned with three tubes.

First he held up the Colgate. "Memsahib," he said, flashing his bright toothy smile a bit longer than necessary, "this kinds—no holes." The he opened his mouth really wide and ran his fingers along his thirty-two perfect teeth. The Sherpas are known for having good straight white teeth and no cavities.

After Nima was sure I had gotten the full impact, he put the Colgate down and picked up the tube of Ultra Brite. "This kinds," he said, breaking out into another unnecessarily long grin, "white teeths." At that point Nima noticed that his omelet was sizzling in the pan, so he quickly put down the Ultra Brite and picked up the tube of Close-up. "This kinds make mouth good smell." With that, he uncapped the tube and ran it by my nose so I could enjoy a good whiff.

For Nima, it was as uncomplicated as that. He didn't appear to be the least bit annoyed at my prying. In fact, he seemed pleased that he had the opportunity to share some of the inside dope with me, in the hopes that I too could have no holes, whiter teeth, and fresher breath. I was about to tell Nima that he had been royally taken, but then I stopped myself. I just didn't have the heart to disillusion him.

Nor did I have the right to. I found myself in my own bathroom taking a shelf count of the products I bought because of something I had seen on TV. On my top shelf, I had five different kinds of hair-care products. There was a shampoo to get rid of the frizzies, another to get rid of the greasies, another to put life back into unexciting hair, and another that had the fragrance of green apples; and there was a creme rinse that smelled like stale strawberries. John claimed that if I ever wore the green-apple shampoo with the strawberry rinse, I would give off the distinct odor of a rancid fruit cup.

Although I was a consumer, I was a conscious one. That was the big difference between Nima and me. I probably owed it to the sponsors and ad agencies to drop them a line telling them how successful they were with Nima, a virgin mind, untouched until a month ago by TV. I could have told them that there were thousands more unsuspecting suckers just like Nima sitting around in the Solu Khumbu near Mount Everest—consumers waiting to happen. From an advertising point of view, Nima might be considered a prime candidate. He had no reason to doubt the validity of those overly sincere voices that talked to him so candidly about Anacin with extra pain relif, Geritol every day, and Preparation-H. To Nima, these could become as important for everyday suburban survival as pitons, crampons, and ropes were on the rugged mountain terrain.

The closest Nima had come to video before he arrived in Connecticut were mountain-climbing films shown to him by Mountain Travel. Several times a year, when the Sherpas gathered to watch the films that instructed them in modern climbing techniques, no one had to tell them to pay close attention. Every Sherpa guide was well aware that the more knowledge gathered from the Australian, British, American, German, and Japanese films, the more he would be able to cope with critical situations. It could mean the difference between life and death. A Sherpa guide was in a profession that required more than courage and strength. It required skill, precision, and the ability to make intelligent, split-second decisions that affected an entire climbing team. If a Sherpa guide didn't take his job seriously, it would eventually take him, and those depending on him.

Nima had his share of close brushes with death. On one Everest expedition an avalanche literally flattened his camp on the western cwm, the level plateau that sits on top of the ice fall.

At the age of fourteen, Nima had already lost several close friends. But that never stopped him. On the Indian Army expedition up Mount Kangchenjunga, Nima had dug in his crampons on a precarious slope. His feet skidded out from under him, sending him into an uncontrollable slide down over a thousand feet, with forty-five pounds on his back. Nima was lucky; he was only dazed and bruised. When he finally did see the training films, he took them seriously. What was there in front of his eyes on the screen was vividly real. It was the truth, the whole truth, and nothing but the truth. To him, the television screen in Connecticut demanded as much respect. Anything that appeared on it just *had* to be true. And that was that.

Of course there were some commercials that influenced Nima more than others. On the top of that list was the commercial in which Sir Edmund Hillary was in front of a Himalayan backdrop extolling the virtues of American Express credit cards. At the end of the plug, Sir Edmund holds up his American Express card and commands, "Don't leave home without it."

That was all Nima needed to hear—Sir Edmund Hillary, supposedly on Nima's home ground somewhere in the Solu

Khumbu, giving a *direct order* to him not to "leave home without it." Sir Edmund is a hero, a god, to all Sherpas. He has built hospitals, bridges, clinics, and schools in the Himalayas. In short, Hillary has dedicated his life to the advancement of the Sherpas.

Immediately after Nima heard Hillary's command, he went to John and said, "Sahib, Nima go store. Buy American Express credit card."

John did not react. He just sat there staring at Nima as if he couldn't register what Nima had just said.

"Nima," I said, "you can't buy an American Express credit card."

Nima looked back at me as if I had spent the last thirty years in a cave. "Memsahib," he said. "Sir Edmund Hillary on TV say *no leave home without it*."

I explained to Nima that this was just a commercial. I told him in a thousand different ways that there was no way he could qualify for a card. It didn't matter that Nima was unaware of what the card was for. The only thing that mattered was that his hero made an explicit command, several times a day, not to leave home without it. Nima was not about to argue with Sir Edmund Hillary.

And even if Nima were to argue with some of the more ludicrous commercials the advertisers were still light years ahead of Nima. By the time a commercial was aired, exhaustive market research had tested the product's effectiveness. Nima just didn't have a chance.

The commercials were only one potentially troublesome aspect of television. They first attracted Nima because they were so simple to grasp—they were short, concise, snappy, catchy, to the point. It didn't take a great mind to figure them out. Many of them were accompanied by a jingle that would stick in the head long after you wished you could forget it. Nima drove us both crazy going around the house, singing and humming everything from Budweiser's "you said it all" to American Airlines' "doin' what we do best." In fact, once Nima got started on them, John and I would unconsciously pick up on the tune and finish where Nima left off.

But as John and I were becoming more and more concerned with Nima's annoying obsession with commercials, another force had slowly been consuming him.

# FIVE

WHEN I FIRST NOTICED this abrupt behavioral change in Nima, I blamed it on homesickness. I knew that Nima missed his family, especially his mother. Several times since Nima's arrival, he had nightmares that his mother was sick and calling out to him for help. The dreams bothered him as much as his mother's sad look when he left Phakding for the United States. The last thing she said was that she would die if anything ever happened to her son. Nima confided that he was his mother's favorite, because he treated her the best. They always did a lot of things together. Sometimes they would go to the weekly trading bazaar in Namche, or see relatives in Thami, or just go to the local festivals. Nima said that they always had a good time because they both laughed at the same things.

We had met Nima's mother at the tiny village of Phakding along the trail. The night before we arrived there, a five day's trek from the base of Mount Everest, Nima had slipped away from his tent without telling us. He ran three hours in the dark, mountainous terrain to warn his mother that we would be arriving the following morning.

We arrived at the ten-thousand-foot-high village

*Nima's mother, sister, and brother in front of a temple on a rare visit to Kathmandu (a two-week trek from their home in Phakding).*

promptly at noon. We had been on the trail for six hours without a break. I had wanted to stop several times, but Mingma hurried us along, saying he didn't want to keep Nima's mother waiting.

The entire village consisted of five houses. Nima was clearly a very important member of the village. Sherpa guides were highly respected even among their own people. The guides are chosen by expedition outfitters after they have proven outstanding courage, strength, and physical endurance. As Nima pointed out, "No scared Sherpa climb up Ice Fall." Nima carried a rather dog-eared certificate that proved he had been an Ice Fall porter and climbed to twenty-four thousand feet without oxygen on the Chris Bonnington assault on Everest.

Nima, who preceded us to his home by half a day, helped his mother prepare our lunch. When he spotted us approaching, he ran to meet us and led us back, introducing us to a few of the Phakding locals along the way. I didn't understand what Nima was telling them about us, but they were listening with great interest, nodding their heads in unison. After Nima exhausted them with information on John and me, he began showing the children a few sleight-of-hand magic tricks that John had taught him only days earlier. The magic show was probably as much for our benefit as theirs. But we both had to admit that Nima did a reasonably good "French drop" using a Nepalese coin. His disappearing-cigarette trick, however, needed work.

After the magic show, he proudly led John and me up a dirt path to a two-story mud-and-stone structure that looked something like a Connecticut barn. We entered through a low, narrow doorway. Once inside, it was pitch black. I could feel straw under my feet, and a lingering aroma of yak dung silently announced that we really were in a barn. Nima told us that the yaks were with his father on a trading caravan to Tibet.

As we climbed up a dark stairway, I grabbed onto the back of John's parka, ducked my head, and blindly followed the others up to the living quarters. Nima's mother greeted us at the top of the stairs. She was dressed in the typical Sherpa costume, a long, dark skirt and a blouse made from a heavy woven wool. The whole ensemble was topped off with a colorful apron, embroidered in a pattern similar to an American Indian motif. The heavy labor, combined with severe weather conditions, did not exactly help preserve a youthful appearance. But Nima's mother was attractive in spirit and humor. Her rigorous life-style did not deter from this. In fact, it almost seemed to have added some sort of inner spiritual glow.

*Nima's mother,* second from left, *and sister,* second from right, *talking with trekkers in front of their home.*

We took off our boots after entering the living quarters and then bowed namaste. Nima's mother went over to a large caldron resting on a brazier in the center of the room and stirred something that looked like grain and water. Nima began pointing out all the features of a Sherpa house. Along one wall was a rough-hewn mantle. Resting on the mantle were artfully molded copper bowls, plates, and cups. We later learned that these Tibetan utensils were a sign of wealth.

Off to one corner of the room was a small altar. It consisted of a picture of Lord Buddha and six yak-butter candles. Nima said that twice a day—before breakfast and dinner—they lighted the candles, burned incense, and prayed to Buddha. I asked what they prayed for. Nima said that usually it was just to say thank you for the food and for their health.

Just then Nima's mother joined us in front of the altar. I gathered that Nima must have asked his mother what she prayed for, because after a few moments of rapid talking, Nima tenderly draped his arm around his mother's shoulder and interpreted. "Mother pray for son Nima every times he leave Phakding."

The tour of Nima's house continued. He pointed to a far corner and said that the entire family slept on mats in the same room. But his mother and father had the most private corner, where they could be tucked away from their four children.

I suddenly realized why it was unusually quiet: Mingma was not around. Nima told us that he had gone down to wash up at the Dudh Khosi River, which was not far from the village. That could have only meant one thing: Nima had a good-looking sister.

Just before lunch was served, Nima's sister emerged at the top of the stairs. She was carrying a large pitcher of chang. Clamped tightly on her heels was Mingma. His hair was carefully slicked to one side and greased with an awful-smelling tonic. His clothes were squeaky clean. In fact he was so well scrubbed from the icy waters that he actually shone. Mingma had gone to a lot of trouble to impress Nima's sister. And I can't say I blamed him. She was *quite* beautiful. But she clearly didn't appear to be the least bit interested in Mingma's conspicuous flirtation.

We were told that whenever you're a guest in a Sherpa home, it is not enough to have one glass of chang. You must have three or four for good luck. In fact, if you really want to show that you're having a good time, then you drink until you drop. John didn't care for the taste of chang. I liked it, but I still couldn't finish more than one glass—especially with Nima's mother topping off my glass after each sip. After the chang, but before lunch, I took out my

Polaroid and asked them if they would like to have their picture taken.

Nima's mother and sister got up and went over to a large chest in the corner of the room. They began pulling out various pieces of clothing and jewelry. For twenty minutes they arranged and rearranged their hair, clothes, and Tibetan jewelry to prepare for the photos.

When everyone was finally ready, Nima played director. He told them exactly where to stand and where to keep their hands. Everyone took Nima's direction, except for Mingma. He remained pasted against Nima's sister. With everyone perfectly posed, Nima slipped in next to his mother. It reminded me of a Grant Wood American Gothic painting. As soon as each print came out, Nima waved his hand over the top of the developing photo. As he did, he said some hocus-pocus that he had picked up from John. Everyone watched the picture form as if Nima were truly Merlin the Magician. Everyone, that is, with the exception of Mingma. His eyes never left Nima's sister.

Although John and I didn't understand one word of the conversation during our lunch, I felt completely at home. The laughter and warmth were infectious. John and I joined in, although we were speaking to Nima's family in English, while they were speaking Sherpa. At moments I felt as if we had transcended the language barrier and actually understood each other. Perhaps it was the chang that kept the words flowing. But more likely it was the affection the Sherpa people showed toward each other and toward strangers that created an irresistible spiritual bond.

At the time of Nima's strange behavior in Connecticut, I reminded him of our visit to his home and how special we thought his family was. But now, Nima had little if anything to say about them. Then I thought, if Nima was indeed homesick, the memories I was conjuring up were just making it worse. The next two nights, I dropped all discussion of what could be bothering him.

But several days later, Nima was not only continuing to act oddly, but he was beginning to show signs of losing his appetite. In the past Nima had eaten as if he had just completed a five-day survival course. Now, he was pushing his food from one corner of his plate to the other. Maybe, I thought, Nima was having some sort of a reaction to his medicine. (When Nima first went on the medication, Dr. Altbaum had told me to watch him closely for signs of a reaction.)

I could no longer remain silent. I quizzed Nima on every aspect of his health. I asked him if he felt nauseated, tired, weak, short of breath, dizzy. But Nima kept answering no. I would have been suspicious of Nima's emphatic no's, had I not just taken him to Dr. Altbaum days before for his regular checkup. Dr. Altbaum was pleased. He told me that he was very encouraged with Nima's steady progress. Soon Nima could begin socializing. He wouldn't need to be spending most of his time in bed. And before long, he could even start school.

I was especially glad to hear that Nima could begin socializing soon. We had purposely been keeping Nima away from our friends, not because he was contagious but because he *looked* contagious. Although Nima had gained ten pounds, he still had a hacking cough. John and I felt that if we waited until Nima gained a little more weight and stopped coughing before we exposed him to our friends, they would have no reason to avoid him. Sherpas are very sensitive, and we didn't want to chance hurting Nima's feelings.

When a few of our friends who had warned us about

bringing Nima here learned that he had TB and was confined to a month of bed rest, they just nodded their heads, as if to say, "We told you so." I can't say that I really blamed them. They didn't know Nima. But I was sure of one thing: the moment they met him, they would take to him just as John and I had. Then they would see that he wasn't slaughtering goats in our living room. In many ways he was more "civilized" than we were.

Though Nima was on the mend, I was still worried about him. I was beginning to run out of theories as to what had triggered his sudden withdrawal. John couldn't come up with any explanation either. The only possibility I could come up with went like this: When active people are suddenly confined to bed rest for a prolonged period they begin to act strangely, almost retreating from the real world. For the last month, Nima had been doing nothing but lying in bed watching TV and occasionally bicycling down to the corner grocery store. This type of limited activity, especially for a Sherpa guide, might just be enough to trigger odd behavior patterns.

If that were the case, then I would just have to remind Nima of what Dr. Altbaum had said on his last visit: in a few short weeks, Nima would be strong enough to go to school and resume a completely normal schedule.

A few days later, Nima was still sullen and withdrawn. I reminded him that he would soon be well enough to start school, but he just sat mutely. I looked over at John for his reaction. John was still nodding his head in agreement with what I had just told Nima. I said, "Are you looking forward to school, Nima?"

"Nima *no go school,*" he said. Then he matter-of-factly placed his knife and fork in the finished position and stood up. In one neat move John reached over, planted a firm hand on Nima's shoulder, and gently pushed him down again.

"What's this not going to school business?" John asked.

From the way Nima flinched and opened his eyes so I could see the whites for the first time in days, I took it he recognized that John was not Captain Kangaroo, nor would he play any more games of "I've Got a Secret."

"Out with it, Nima," John said.

Nima spilled his guts out. "Nima *no* good. Nepal *no* good. Sherpa *no* good. Solu Khumbu *no* good. Memsahib good. Sahib good. America good. Nima *no* good."

Then he retreated to his room and closed the door behind him. John started after him, but before he got to Nima's door he threw up his hands, turned around, and came back to the table.

As I looked over at Nima's half-eaten dinner and then across the room to his closed bedroom door, I tried putting myself in his shoes to see if I could come up with a reason he was saying all those "no good" things about himself and his country.

John and I agreed on one thing: it had to be something pretty serious to provoke him into self-denigration. The only negative thing I had ever heard Nima say about the Solu Khumbu was something to the effect that if the Sherpas weren't careful, they would soon be overrun with the Tamang and Khamba tribes.

Maybe, I thought, someone had said something about the Solu Khumbu to deflate his ego. But the more I thought about someone saying something like that to Nima, the more unlikely it seemed.

I looked at my watch. It was now over an hour since Nima had stalked off to his bedroom. We were still hoping that he would come out and explain what he meant by

71

"Nima no good." But Nima obviously was in no rush to explain anything. John and I were left with no choice but to get to the root of the problem once and for all. We would have an immediate confrontation.

John knocked. Nima immediately appeared at the door. It was almost as if he had wondered what had taken us so long.

"Come in, Sahib, Memsahib," Nima said, his eyes locked on the TV.

"Nima," John said, "Liz and I want to know why you said you're no good."

Nima appeared to be more intent on looking at the TV than coming up with an answer. I thought he hadn't heard John, because the TV was too loud.

John got up turned off the TV, came back to the sofa, and repeated the question—this time about ten decibels louder.

We got Nima's undivided attention. Whether it was because of John's raised voice or Nima's shock at seeing the TV go black just before "MASH" was about to go on the air, I couldn't say. When we got our answer, we became more confused than ever.

Nima reluctantly began. "Every night times Nima look 'MASH.' Every night times Nima see good peoples."

Nima looked over at John, then me, then back to the blank screen.

"Good people look same like Memsahib, same like Sahib. Sahib look same like B.J. Memsahib look same like Hot Lip Hoolihan."

I guess Nima really did think all Americans looked alike. I nodded, as if I agreed with him.

"All good people," he continued, "try help all no-good people. No-good people look same like Nima. Same like boss Lhakpa. Same like father. Same like brother. Same like uncle in Namche."

John and I sat in silence, stunned. Nima stopped talking only long enough to check his watch for the time. Then he elaborated.

"No-good peoples try kill Hawkeye. Dr. Hawkeye look same like Dr. Altbaum. Other day Hawkeye and Hot Lip go in truck. Take medicines to sick people in village."

Nima's eyes began welling up. John realized that Nima was getting emotional. He looked away from Nima and stared at me as if I had something to do with the script.

Nima went on, "Village look same like Phakding. No-good people come out village tree. Come out village bush. Many peoples carry thing look same like kukri knife. Knife make loud sound. Maybe knife. Maybe gun."

Nima picked up the scissors that he used for cutting out coupons from the newspaper, and he imitated the way the village people attacked. Nima grabbed the tips as if they were a weapon, hopped off the sofa, crouched down, and crawled to the sliding glass door, all the while making a bam, bam, bam sound. Nima appeared all set to crawl back toward the sofa, but John jumped up and grabbed the scissors from Nima before he impaled himself.

When they were both safely back on the sofa, Nima continued. "Village no-good people take Hot Lip, take Hawkeye to house. House same like uncle teahouse."

Nima stopped again, this time to ask us if we remembered his uncle's teahouse in Namche Bazaar. That was one visit we would never forget. First, his aunt and uncle loaded us up with *dahlbaat,* the Nepalese dish of rice, curry, and lentils. Then they pushed about four glasses of chang on us, and insisted on showing us Sherpa dances. We danced until we dropped.

"No-good man look same like uncle. Man tie Hot Lip, tie Hawkeye feets and hand. Hot Lip cry. Hawkeye say, 'No cry, Hot Lip.' No-good man no care Hot Lip cry. No-good man go out to truck. Steal medicines. Hawkeye go like *this* with mouths."

Nima put his wrist to his mouth to show us how Hawkeye was able to chew away the rope.

"Hawkeye good teeths. Hawkeye get Hot Lip no rope. Hawkeye, Hot Lip go like snake to truck. No-good man no see."

As Nima was telling us of the episode, he was clearly reliving their near-death. Nima ended his drama by telling us that Hot Lips and Hawkeye escaped. But Nima also warned us that Hawkeye's and Hot Lips's luck could not last forever.

As Nima continued to chronicle the "MASH" version of the Korean War, John continued staring at me. I knew John wanted me to interrupt Nima's narrative, but I felt it would be good therapy for him to spill it all out. It wasn't easy, though, to understand how a simple sitcom could have such an effect on Nima.

"Nima," I said, "'MASH' is just a show." But Nima was thousands of miles away, off in some Korean base camp watching over Hot Lips, Hawkeye, and the rest of the "MASH" unit.

Then it suddenly hit me. Nima didn't know that "MASH" was just a show. He thought it was real. John and I had never told Nima that some of the shows on TV are real and some are not. It never occurred to us. We just assumed he would know. But there was nothing in his background for him to recognize what was real and what wasn't on the TV screen. He had only seen those climbing films at Mountain Travel. He had never even been to a movie.

Nima's behavior was slowly making sense to me. No wonder he had watched "MASH" so steadily over the last month. He was probably waiting to see if the North Koreans, who looked like Nima and his family, would ever do anything commendable. They never seemed to.

Again I attempted to get Nima's attention. I leaned over and gently shook his arm. "Nima, 'MASH' is *not* real."

"'MASH' no real?" Nima said. His eyes focused on me, but they were full of confusion.

John repeated what I had just said. Then I repeated what John had said. And Nima repeated what we both had said, "'MASH' no real?"

"That's right," I said. "'MASH'" is just a game. Hawkeye, Hot Lips, B.J., Radar, Klinger—they are all getting paid lots of money to pretend to be good."

"Hawkeye," John said, pointing toward the blank TV screen, "is not a doctor. He's not like Dr. Altbaum. He's an actor."

I reminded John that Nima didn't know about actors. Then I tried to explain the concept of acting. The best I could do was to relate our Hollywood actors to his monks and lamas, who at festival time dress up in bright costumes and wear large papier-mâché masks as they dance around the monastery courtyard performing acts of good and evil.

"Hawkeye and Hot Lips," I said, "are like the monks and lamas at Tengboche festival time." I was quite pleased with my brilliant analogy. That is until I saw Nima's eyes open wide in disbelief.

"Hot Lip, Hawkeye same like lama?" Nima asked. Then he slapped his palm against his forehead and began talking to himself in Sherpa.

"The people who look like you," I said, "are supposed to be North Koreans. They're actors too."

"Liz is right," John said. "Everyone you see on 'MASH' is an actor."

Nima was sitting stone upright. Although his body looked as if rigor mortis had set in, his face looked as if the weight of the Orient had been lifted from it.

"No-good peoples," Nima asked, "same like father, same like uncle, same like Nima, *no* try kill Hawkeye, Hot Lip?"

"That's right, Nima. It's all a game," I said.

"Why Hawkeye, Hot Lip no try kill no-good peoples?"

"Because that's not how the producers want the game played." Then I realized that Nima didn't know about producers. So I explained that a producer was sort of like Mingma. They both handled the money, made the rules, bossed people around, and in the end they both creamed off the big bucks.

But Nima wasn't interested in producers. He was strictly interested in the "MASH" unit, and especially Hot Lips, Hawkeye, and B.J.

"No-good peoples, *no* hate Hot Lip, Hawkeye, B.J.?"

I felt Nima was now asking just so he could hear John and me confirm the good news, I certainly couldn't fault him for that. John and I were more than ready to repeat as many times as he wanted to hear that the people who looked like him were really good.

"Nima," I said "the people who look like Sherpas are called Koreans. They are very, very good people. But I think the producer believes that it makes a much better game if they pretend to be no-good."

I wasn't giving Nima the whole truth, but I couldn't think of any civilized way to tell him that if the North Koreans ever turned out to be the good guys, the whole "MASH" staff would be collecting food stamps. However, I did tell Nima that all the actors probably ate lunch in the same commissary, went to a lot of the same parties, and even shared the same wardrobe designers.

By the end of the evening Nima was his old self. And that old self was no longer too troubled to eat. He removed a box of doughnuts from his desk drawer. After he offered John and me one, he proceeded to down one after the other, until the box was emptied, crumbs and all. Then he carefully folded the box and returned it to the desk drawer. I told Nima that he was wasting his time—there is no return deposit on doughnut boxes. But Nima explained that he was saving the box because the girls down at Peter's had pointed out that on the back of that box was a coupon that would get him twenty-five cents off the purchase price on his next box of doughnuts. There was also a special offer for a sports wallet.

That's when Nima showed me his top desk drawer. It was full of coupons, so many that if I hadn't been confident of Nima's integrity, I would have thought he had been mugging little old ladies for their handbags. Nima told me that the girls at the market *always* saved coupons for him because they weren't allowed to let him bargain them down from the label price.

Along with his appetite came a renewed sense of dignity. After we had explained to Nima all about actors and how "MASH" was just a game, we listened to him explain to us that the more he thought about those North Koreans on "MASH," the more they looked just like the Tamangs; and that it was foolish on his part to think that they even *slightly* resembled the Sherpas. Nima didn't let it drop at that. He gave us a complete rundown on the differences between the Sherpas and the North Koreans, as opposed to the similarities between the Tamangs and the North Koreans. He said something to the effect that the North Koreans, like the Tamangs, were small, weak, "no brave," and that he'd like to just once see one of them climb as high as Phakding.

That night, John and I went to bed mystified. We couldn't figure out how the information we programmed into Nima's computer about "MASH," producers, Nielsen ratings, and even wardrobe designers could have been translated back into "the Tamangs and Koreans are both losers."

John was convinced that Nima didn't understand anything of what we had spent an hour and a half telling him. But I felt he had. It was just that Nima was expressing himself the only way he knew how: taking his frustration and confusion out on his personal whipping boys, the Tamangs and Khambas, helped elevate his own self-worth. I could see a part of Nima in me, a part that I tried desperately not to expose.

As it turned out, Nima did understand that "MASH" was not real. But along with that, he also assumed that everything on TV was not real; it was all a game. I discovered that the next morning when I came down for breakfast.

Nima greeted me in the kitchen with a namaste, *The New York Times,* and the widest smile I had ever seen. Then he went over to the cupboard and helped himself to his second bowl of cereal. We chatted very briefly, because Nima appeared anxious to get back to his room. On his way out he grabbed a banana and reminded himself that he had to return a bad banana to Peter's Market. Balancing the cereal in one hand and a glass of milk in the other, he explained that he had to hurry back for a good show—and he left.

I thought to myself: what kind of a good show could be on at 7:15 in the morning? In light of the previous night's drama, I decided to find out.

I went to Nima's room to remind him that he had a doctor's appointment at one o'clock. But Nima already had it written down in the pocket diary John had given him. Nima told me to stay right where I was, because after the commercial I might see a helicopter just like the kind on "MASH" and the kind at Lukla airstrip being shot down.

Nima was watching the "Today Show." The news of the day was the Russian invasion of Afghanistan. An English correspondent came on the screen, direct from the war zone. He was surrounded by heavy artillery and men dressed in battle fatigues. Nima pointed to the screen and said, "Actor get many moneys?"

With that, I understood. Nima thought that the NBC news was a sitcom just like "MASH."

"Nima," I said, "this is real. It is not like 'MASH.'

"Real?" Nima asked. "No game?"

Because I didn't know what to say to Nima about war I said nothing. In turn, Nima asked nothing, other than if I was *sure* that it wasn't just a game. I was almost tempted to tell him it was all a game and then rip out both television sets. Every day after that, every time a show came on the air, Nima would come and get either John or me and ask us if the show was real or if it was a game.

John and I decided that it was about time for Nima to get some outside interests. What we didn't realize was that one of those new outside interests would eventually change Nima's life forever.

# SIX

GROVER MILLS WAS AN AMERICAN born and bred in Westport, Connecticut—a far cry from Nima Dorje Sherpa, who
was born and bred in the foothills of Mount Everest. But on
the cool October morning when Nima first bowed namaste
to Grover, and Grover reciprocated with a Pittsburgh
Steeler-type handshake, it was the beginning of a new union. For Nima, Grover would soon become next in line to
Sir Edmund Hillary. And for Grover, Nima would soon
become the little brother he never had.

Nima had two missions in life. One was to become a
senior Sherpa guide, just like Mingma. The other was to
build a teahouse, just like Mingma's. The teahouse had been
a passion of Nima's for reasons I could only guess at. I
suppose it had a lot to do with the fact that Mingma owned
a teahouse in Kathmandu. Sherpas are quietly aggressive. A
successful Sherpa not only is a mountain guide, which is
prestigious in itself, but he often owns a house, land, and
yaks. And very successful Sherpas, such as Mingma, own a
teahouse.

Nima had told us about the teahouse back in the
Himalayas when he showed us the logs he had laboriously
cut and stored near his house at Phakding. A teahouse along

the trail to the high Tibetan passes is a small, elongated shack with a cozy fire in an open pit, a few rough-hewn tables and benches, lit by bronze bowls and burning yak butter. There are two or three bunk rooms for weary yak-caravan traders or European trekkers who come in from the blustering winds that sweep down from Everest.

Nima had many logs ready, but not half enough. He had his dreams, though.

Grover had his dreams, too. For years, he had been thinking of trekking through the Himalayas, a dream that resurfaced the moment he met Nima.

I suppose what drew the two of them together more quickly than anything was that each had a background that complemented the other. For Nima, Grover was an ace carpenter who not only held the knowledge but the tools that could shape Nima's dream. And for Grover, Nima was an expert climber from the roof of the world, which he had only dreamed of standing on. But there was another even more important reason why Grover would soon take Nima under his wing.

After graduating from college, Grover had taught junior high school biology for a while, and then along with his wife, Kerrie, he took off for the mountains of Chile with the Peace Corps. Together they covered the steep slopes of the Andes on horseback. Both became deeply moved by the plight of the Chilean villagers. Both developed love and respect for the mountain people.

It was the middle of October when Grover and his men began lifting the roof of our attic to make an additional bedroom. Everything was going well. Dr. Altbaum kept giving us one optimistic report after another on Nima's health. He claimed that he had never seen anyone recover so rapidly from a serious illness. If John and I had planned it, we could not have arranged a more perfect time for Nima and Grover to meet. At first we couldn't keep Nima away from the TV, but now we couldn't keep Nima away from watching Grover and his carpenters at work. The vision of his teahouse was obviously growing in his mind. Soon he was scrambling after nails and lumber for Grover and acting as an all-round volunteer. His enthusiasm was barely short of startling.

Nima had been a go-fer for only a week before Grover recognized that he was apprentice material. Nima appeared to have more energy than ever. From 8:30 A.M. to 4:30 P.M. he was Grover's carpenter. He was now also unofficially on Grover's payroll. Nima's day began at 7:00 with the TV news. By 8:00, he had had his usual two breakfasts. And by 8:20, Nima had a thermos filled with steaming coffee for Grover and his men. By 8:30 Nima was outside, perched on the steps, waiting for the trucks to pull up. Nima had only one complaint: three out of five mornings, Grover showed up anywhere from ten minutes to an hour and twenty minutes late. Before going on Grover's payroll, Nima let the tardiness slip by unnoticed. But now that Nima was getting paid from the moment Grover arrived, he could no longer look the other way. In no uncertain terms, Nima told Grover what Mingma did to guides who showed up late— even the first time.

Once Nima's attention had been diverted from TV he became a productive human being, both mentally and physically. He not only found time to resume letterwriting to his family, but to Mingma as well. In fact, for every two letters to his mother, Mingma got one. Of course the letters to his mother were always in Tibetan characters, whereas those for Mingma were always in English, always dictated to me and always with the intention that Mingma would have to ask Big Boss Lhakpa for the translation. Mingma

*Grover Mills and Nima at a construction site in Connecticut.*

couldn't read one word of English, and Nima knew that
Mingma didn't have a friend who could translate. Mingma
would be left with no choice but to go their boss, Lhakpa,
for the translation.

By writing the letter to Mingma in English, Nima would
indirectly impress Lhakpa with his wordliness, bravery,
courage, and strength. Lhakpa would see that Nima would
be a very likely candidate for promotion to sirdar, a position
that Mingma held. At the same time, Mingma would be
eating his heart out over Nima's good fortune. Nima said
that he was sure Mingma would take the letter to Lhakpa
because of his greed to find out if he bought the "cow-hat
and boot" that he had requested.

The last time Nima had written to Mingma was days
after he had gotten out of the hospital. At that time he had
told Mingma that the hospital in America looked "same like

Rana Palace," and that all the doctors looked "same like New Zealand doctor." There were no Spirit A-Tutu doctors at the Norwalk Hospital. But they were still very good. He told Mingma that all the doctors and nurses said, "Nima many braves. Nima no cry. Nima no scared, skinny chicken." The very last thing he dictated was that very soon he would be looking for the "cow-hat and boot." Now, months later, he had real news for Mingma.

To Mingma:
Daily best wishes. Nima two week work with Grover. Nima get 84 big ones. House in America no look same like Namche. House have many room, many toilet, many glass, many water. Wood same like Sherpa house. Nima cut many woods. Grover say Tamang and Khamba cut all finger off try cut woods with Black and Decker.

Grover and Nima go deli for bagel and egg for lunch times. Tomorrow Grover teach Nima make fireplace. America fireplace much good. No smokes in house. Grover say Nima fast learn. Good carpenter. Grover say Tamang no learn like Sherpa learn. Memsahib better cooks than all Khumbu. Memsahib cook good noodle, good vegetable, good lettuce, good ice creams. Everything goods.

Nima, Memsahib, Sahib go party every night times. America peoples all good, all riches. Rich no like Mingma. Rich same like Rana. No hard works. No pick potato. No yak. Just many, many moneys. Nima go school tomorrow after tomorrow.

Sahib, Memsahib say Nima same like son. Nima say Memsahib, Sahib, same like mother, same like father. Namaste for Lhakpa. Nima look for find Mingma cow-hat and boot next week after next week. Much for now.

You friend,
Namaste, Nima Dorje Sherpa

If I hadn't insisted on cutting Nima's letter short, we probably would have ended up with a full-length piece of fiction. Several times during his dictation I stopped and asked that he keep as close to the facts as possible. I told Nima that it wouldn't be logical for Grover to slander the Tamangs and Khambas. Grover never even heard of those tribes before. I also told Nima that he was using words that Mingma would not understand. Mingma wouldn't know that "big ones"— a phrase Grover used—meant dollars, or that a Black and Decker was a power saw, that a deli was a restaurant and a bagel was bread. But Nima insisted that I leave all the buzzwords in and let Mingma worry about what they meant.

I knew that Nima was probably flattering me when he brought up my cuisine, the same way he was impressing Mingma with his wordliness and Big Boss Lhakpa with his extraordinary skill as a carpenter and all-around brilliant person. But it was when Nima got to the part about John and me saying he was just like our son and we were just like his parents that I was truly touched.

Before Nima arrived, John and I had agreed that, whatever we did, we would be careful not to build a thick emotional bond with Nima. It was inevitable that six months later the bond would have to be wrenched apart. Nima's departure would then be as difficult for him as it would be for us. In theory it was a good idea; in actuality it was destined never to work.

From that warm September day that Nima was helped off the Air India plane and handed over to us, we were hooked. We were more than emotionally hooked. We were realistically bound, bound to the reality that whatever happened to Nima would be a direct result of what we did. Or what we didn't do. And at that time, it did not look good.

*Nima's passport picture, taken in Kathmandu shortly before he came to stay with us in Connecticut. He weighed about 85 pounds.*

*Nima in Connecticut after treatment for tuberculosis. At 135 pounds, he is healthy and robust.*

He was so fragile we weren't sure he would make it. If the worst happened, we would have to live with that the rest of our days.

Nima was hooked on us as well. We were all he had—in this hemisphere, at least. All his trust had been transferred to John and me. Now when I think back to the sight of Nima that day at Kennedy Airport, I'm ashamed of what I thought. I thought that John and I had made the biggest mistake of our lives. Fortunately, we were proved wrong. Nima's visit was fast turning out to be an extremely positive experience. Dr. Altbaum couldn't get over Nima's recuperative ability. And Grover said about Nima's carpentry talent, "The kid is a natural." Before long Nima was headed for another positive experience. This time in the classroom.

Staples High School entered Nima's life three weeks after Grover Mills. The morning of registration, Nima disappeared into his room right after breakfast. Following a half-hour under the shower, and more time in front of the mirror blow-drying his straight, black hair, he emerged. And when he did, he was in style. Before I actually saw him, I got one nose-piercing whiff. Drenched in Brut aftershave—a bargain he had picked up for half price down at the Weston pharmacy because the cap was damaged—he smelled like one of those women who embalm themselves in perfume and invariably take the seat next to you on the bus.

He was wearing a brand-new pair of Levi's, a Western riding shirt, a jean jacket with the cuffs turned up just once in a very casual fashion. The whole ensemble was topped off with a red bandana that the sales clerk threw in because he couldn't take anything more off the sale price. He had given up explaining to Nima that uneven stitching did not warrant a discount.

On the way to Staples, a ten-minute ride through the Westport–Weston winding roads, I reassured Nima that Mr. Tata, the director of the evening school program, was a very good man, and that he shouldn't be anxious about the meeting.

"Mr. Tata," Nima said somewhat nervously from the back seat, "same like Sir Edmund Hillary?"

I explained to Nima that Mr. Tata didn't actually build the high school as Sir Edmund had built all the Sherpa schools. He was, however, in charge of all the teachers, as well as the courses. I didn't blame Nima for being a little apprehensive. John and I had met Sir Edmund back in the Himalayas, completely by accident. I got so excited when he joined us at our campsite for lunch that I had a hard time getting words out. John did most of the talking.

Mr. Tata told John over the phone that when he first meets foreign-speaking students, nine times out of ten they are reluctant to talk. That, he said, makes it very difficult to discern at which level of English the student should be placed. To avoid that with Nima, John and I encouraged him not to hold back the conversation when he met with Mr. Tata. As we walked through the parking lot and up to the school's entrance I reminded Nima of that. I also reminded him just to act naturally.

I never expected Nima to act quite so naturally, though. When Mr. Tata asked him if he had had any schooling in the Himalayas, and if so how many years, Nima straightened his Fairfield Lumber baseball cap and answered in his newly acquired Grover accent, "Yup, four big ones."

I nudged Nima, but it did little good. He continued to drop "big ones" into the conversation. Each time he did Mr. Tata's eyes widened as if he wasn't sure he had heard him correctly.

In spite of the slang, Mr. Tata appeared more than mildly amused at Nima's willingness to talk. In fact, he encouraged Nima to carry on—not that Nima needed any encouragement. Nima told Mr. Tata all about his four years at the Hillary school. I was relieved, however, that Nima decided to leave out the part about how he liked to cuff his friends. But he didn't leave out a few of his prejudicial views. He told Mr. Tata that when he went to the Hillary school, no Tamangs or Khambas were there. But now, he said, the place was loaded with them. In between Nima's running dialogue about his school, he told Mr. Tata all about his apprenticeship with Grover, even down to minute details. Nima said that just the day before Grover had reminded him, "Nima no nail foot to floor when toe-nailing stud. Nima many carefuls. Grover *no* careful. Grover and Nima get ready for lunchtimes. But Grover no get up. Grover nail foot to floor."

After Nima shared a few more construction anecdotes with us, I explained why Nima was so enthusiastic over his new job. I told Mr. Tata that Nima had once said no respectable Sherpa would consider becoming a bootmaker or tailor. Such trades are looked down on as unworthy of a Sherpa's talent and are usually practiced by the not-so-successful Khambas, who have little choice but to take on the more menial tasks. On the other hand, carpentry is a whole different story. The Sherpas hold carpenters in high esteem. In fact, they probably run a close second to the village lama. Both the lama and the carpenter are invited into homes to serve very worthwhile functions: the lama rids the Sherpa house of unwanted spirits and the carpenter uses his expertise to build or repair.

When he finally got the chance, Mr. Tata explained to Nima what he would be learning at Staples. From Nima's expression, I could tell that he was excited about starting. I could also tell from the way he glanced down at his Timex once too often that he wished Mr. Tata would get on with it, so he could still get in half a day's work with Grover.

Finally, Mr. Tata handed Nima a first grader's book and asked him if he was able to read any of it. I wasn't surprised when Nima was able to read almost every word. From the time Nima had gotten out of the hospital, we had been spending several hours each week practicing the alphabet and reading and writing simple words.

Nima, more than pleased with himself, handed the book back to Mr. Tata and said, "Mingma no read one words of book."

Mr. Tata now looked totally confused. That was about the third reference to Mingma in less than twenty minutes. "Who is Mingma?" Mr. Tata asked, sliding his glasses down his nose and peering over the rims.

I didn't want Nima to get started, so I began to tell Mr. Tata about Mingma. But before I even got to the part about Mingma's Napoleonic complex, John jabbed me under the table with his clunky boot.

At the end of the interview, Mr. Tata told us that even though Nima seemed to have a fairly good grasp of the English language, he was still going to place him in the beginner's class. He explained that this would be psychologically advantageous, especially in Nima's case. John and I assumed that what he was trying to say was the Nima's ego would be better off at the top of the beginner class, rather than at the bottom of the intermediate.

We thanked Mr. Tata for his time and interest. As we left the office, John and I clasped our hands together, brought them to our faces, and bowed namaste. Mr. Tata did likewise. That was the Sherpa custom I liked the most. Even though it probably looked like an affectation when John and I performed the namaste, we did it anyway.

I turned back to see what was keeping Nima. He was straightening that Fairfield Lumber baseball cap again in the reflection of the window. When he realized that we were ready to leave, he rushed out into the hall to join us. Then John, Mr. Tata, and I bowed namaste one more time. But Nima didn't. Instead, he firmly extended his arm toward Mr. Tata. With his palm turned down and his elbow crooked like a football player, Nima shook his hand and said, "Take it easy, ya hear?" Then he pivoted on his Adidases and led us out of the building.

As we pulled out of the school's parking lot, I couldn't help thinking about the difference between the rather primitive structures Sir Edmund Hillary had built and the modern, sprawled-out, California-style high school Nima would soon be attending. I also thought about the time we had met Hillary.


It was in a village called Junbesi, a settlement at nine thousand feet that rested on a steep cliff over the rushing, icy Beni Khola River—which swept down from the twenty-two-thousand-foot peak called Numbur. As we approached from the heights of the trail, a small monastery glistened in the noonday sun, and a cluster of buildings far below it sat snugly around a religious stupa—a small, dome-shaped monument that raised its spire toward a brilliant blue sky. Although the village's sole means of communication with the outside world was through one narrow footpath that stretched from the Kathmandu Valley to the Nangpa La on the Tibetan border, it somehow did not create a feeling of isolation.

Junbesi was the first place where we could begin our research into the mystique of the Sherpa's Buddhist beliefs, which have such a great influence on their lives. A two-hour trek above the village, high on a mountainous rise, lay the Thubtenchholing Monastery, headed by the abbot who had formerly presided over the Rongbuk Monastery just over the Tibetan border on the other side of Mount Everest. The abbot was reported to speak good English. That was promising, because as good a companion as Nima was, his English was simply not up to philosophical explanations.

All the way down the high pass, my knee was continuing to buckle, to the point where the pain was excruciating. Nima was constantly at my side, offering firm support as we moved closer to Junbesi. With ten days down, and nearly a month to go on the trail, I was beginning to have serious doubts about ever making our destination: the Everest base camp. I was sure that the trail had never been subjected to a more decrepit trekker. At least John was able to hold his own. Although Nima was always patient, he was constantly quizzing us as to exactly what we were doing in the Himalayas. That was the same thing I was beginning to wonder. If I had been honest, I would have admitted to John before we left the United States that I would have preferred two weeks on the Côte d'Azur searching for Michelin two-star restaurants and designer boutiques.

We pitched camp at noon on the river, below the cliff where Junbesi sat. In the village, we found that a runner was leaving for Kathmandu and we were able to scrawl some letters and mail them out; it was our first chance to communicate with the outside world. We wondered, of course, whether they would ever reach their destinations. Weeks later we discovered that they had.

From the village, we could see our target for the next day, the Thubtenchholing Monastery. The trail was shielded to the north by a ten-thousand-foot ridge near the settlement of Mapung. We could, however, see the smaller gomba in Junbesi, sitting directly above the village on a

*Nima,* right, *setting up our tent. In heavy rainstorms, he would dig a trench around the base of the tent.*

steep hill. Since it looked reachable before sunset, we arranged for Mingma to take us up after lunch.

We set out for the monastery with Mingma, Pasang, and Nima. They wanted to stop at a small teahouse along the way, which it turned out, was owned by Mingma's sister. She greeted us warmly and insisted on pouring us glass after glass of chang, typical of Sherpa hospitality. Two sips from a glass, and it was immediately filled up again. Soon, two other Sherpas burst into the tiny room, both from Mountain Travel. Mingma, Pasang, and Nima greeted them like classmates at a college reunion, as the Sherpas always did when they ran into each other on the trail. It wasn't long before the Sherpa dances began.

After nearly an hour in the teahouse, John and I began making gestures indicating that it was time to leave. But Mingma didn't appear to be in any hurry. He was on his

*This is the kind of bridge I* hated. *Nima's kidding around didn't help calm my nerves at all.*

fourth glass of chang. Pasang was trying desperately to keep up with him. It sometimes appeared that all Pasang ever wanted out of life was to be Mingma's best friend. When the two of them were together they treated Nima as if he were the kid brother they were stuck with. And since Nima didn't drink, he was even more excluded from the frivolities.

It was midafternoon before we were able to separate Mingma from the chang. The weather had turned chillier and windier. Although my knee was still bothering me, I felt we should force ourselves to visit the monks in preparation for the trip to the larger monastery on the following day. Mingma estimated that it would take us less than an hour each way, which would get us back into camp by sundown, when the cold would really set in.

Even though we were wary of Mingma's time estimates,

*A lama encountered along the trail looks with pleasure at the Polaroid we took of him. A* mani *wall is in the background.*

we set out, bending against the wind in our parkas, climbing upward and forcing ourselves with every step. Mingma and Pasang, fueled with the chang, were galloping ahead. They did, however, stop at regular intervals for us to catch up. By the time an hour had passed, we seemed no nearer the monastery than when we had started. When an hour and a half had gone by, we still hadn't reached it, and the climb had steepened. We knew now that we would never make it back to the campsite by sundown: we told Mingma we would have to surrender. We retreated, fully aware that we had failed in our first real mission of the journey.

But back in the village on the way to our camp, John noticed three bright blue trekking tents in the little schoolyard and asked Mingma what they were. He explained that Sir Edmund Hillary and his brother Rex were in the area, continuing their work building schools and hospitals for the Sherpa people. There was a strong mutual regard and respect between Sir Edmund and the Sherpas since Hillary and Sherpa Tenzing Norkay had jointly reached the summit of Everest a quarter of a century before.

We stopped by the schoolyard and found Rex Hillary directing a crew of Sherpas constructing a building that would become a badly needed clinic in the area, and also shaping an addition to the school building. Browned by the Himalayan sun, Rex Hillary, a gray-haired, energetic man in his fifties, greeted us cordially, apologizing for the dirt on his coveralls. He told us how he and Sir Edmund were rushing to finish the job here at Junbesi before they went on toward Everest to repair the school and hospital they had built in the high villages of Kunde and Khumjung over a decade before. Sir Edmund would be arriving the following morning from a nearby village where he, too, was helping work crews with a hospital project.

Hillary's dedication to, and projects for, the Sherpa people were widely recognized and we were interested in learning more about them. John asked Rex Hillary if he and Sir Edmund would join us for lunch at our camp the next day, when Sir Edmund was due to arrive. Rex felt sure they could, but would have to confirm it as soon as he learned when his brother would arrive.

The following morning, a runner arrived to tell us that Sir Edmund had accepted our invitation to lunch, along with his brother Rex and two others in his party who were hiking up from Phaphlu that morning. Mingma assured us that there would be plenty of food.

But as lunchtime approached only a few porters were around our campsite. None of them seemed to know where Mingma, Pasang, Nima, and nine porters had gone. None of them knew English, and it was impossible to get any further information. We were concerned because Hillary's time was limited. His brother told us that he had to return to Phaphlu by nightfall, a three-hour hike.

As the appointed time drew near, I looked up toward the cliff that led to the village. There I saw a caravan of our Sherpas and the rest of the porters. They were descending the cliff bearing extra straw chairs, a wide tabletop, a Tibetan rug, and some lovely Oriental teacups and china. It all came from the teahouse that Mingma's sister ran in the village.

Our drab mess tent was transformed into a tent fit for an OPEC sheik. The last-minute touches had barely been completed when we saw Sir Edmund and his party approaching along the riverbank. He was the perfect image of the first man to conquer the world's highest mountain—tall, robust, and craggy, with a face bronzed and creased by years of adventure.

But he was much more than an adventurer. His dedication to the people of Nepal was profound and far-reaching, made possible by a foundation he established, and for which he continues raising funds years after his conquest of Everest.

Mingma, Pasang, and Nima had outdone themselves in making the lunch festive. In fact, Mingma's imperiousness turned into downright obsequiousness. As he offered Sir Edmund *rakshi,* a winelike brandy, he bowed so deeply I was afraid he was going to get his greased hair all over the delicate Tibetan tablecloth. Mingma, Nima, and Pasang shared the honor of serving the various courses.

After the rakshi, Nima swept into the crowded tent smiling so brightly you could almost see his molars. He was carrying a huge platter of boiled yak meat. In moments the platter was empty. But Nima didn't appear to be in any hurry to move from Sir Edmund's side, where he was still

*When Sir Edmund Hillary joined us for lunch along the trail, our Sherpas went all out and served him a four-course feast.*

beaming over at his six-foot four-inch hero, as if in a trance. Mingma put an end to that. From outside the tent flap, I could see him signal Nima that it was time to move.

Next to enter was Pasang. This time the platter was piled high with French fries and apple fritters. Mingma must have warned Pasang not to stand around wearing a glazed expression. He was so rigid, he looked like a wound-up tin soldier; he had virtually no expression on his face. The moment the last fritter was scooped up he was gone, and Mingma entered proudly carrying an artfully decorated tray of hard-boiled eggs, cheese, and something that tasted like a white pound cake with coconut and nuts. It had been made over the open fire.

Although this type of hospitality was not unique for Sir Edmund, he did not take it for granted. As each Sherpa entered, Sir Edmund would acknowledge the lavish courses and chat briefly about their respective villages and families.

During lunch Hillary told us about his projects. His team had been in Nepal about ten days, with Rex and another New Zealand carpenter concentrating on the work at Junbesi, while Sir Edmund concentrated on improving a medical clinic in Phaphlu, which was downriver from where he had walked that morning. Soon they would be moving deeper into the mountains to build urgently needed bridges and to continue improving the medical facilities and schools far up in Kunde, near Everest.

"The problem with Ed is," Rex was saying, "he's never satisfied. We've been working on the clinic here from dawn to dusk. The Sherpas all volunteer their work, just as we do. They haul the timber down from the mountains, all hand-sawn the full length of the trunk, mind you, and then pitch in to help with the construction. But the first thing Ed said to me when he arrived this morning was, 'Haven't you got any farther along than this?' "

After completing the construction of a total of seventeen schools, several hospitals, and numerous bridges, the Hillarys were back for a three-month stint to continue their work. One school, far up in the village of Thami, had literally been blown away in a monsoon storm, and rebuilding it

*Pasang, Nima, and Mingma,* left to right, *standing behind me at Junbesi after our lunch with Sir Edmund Hillary.*

was another project on their schedule. This was no easy job. Lumber had to be carried on the backs of porters, a two-day haul for the volunteer Sherpa carriers. We saw some of them later in the upper forests, bending under a load of heavy, twelve-foot-long timbers held on their backs only by a strap around their foreheads. Timber was scarce in the Khumbu. Centuries of use had stripped away much of the forest land. More and more of the Sherpas were having to turn to dried yak dung as fuel.

"I'm afraid things are changing in the highlands, and lowlands, too," Sir Edmund said. "There will be a strong need for conservation here as well as the rest of the world."

Hillary was careful not to make his projects mere handouts. He keyed his work into what the local people wanted, and they willingly supported him with volunteers.

"In Phaphlu," he said, "we counted up over ten thousand hours of volunteer labor on the part of the Sherpas. They want to help themselves. That's what is so gratifying. The schools are probably our most satisfying endeavor. Sherpas have a great curiosity. They love to learn. The Sherpa children are as good students as any in New Zealand or other parts of the world."

Driving Nima back home from his interview at the high school, I found myself wondering what kind of student Nima would become here on the opposite side of the world in America.

We were soon to find out.

# SEVEN

AT THE END OF OCTOBER, John's English publisher invited us to London for a two-week radio and TV promotion tour of his latest book. But we had a problem—we couldn't leave Nima home alone. I was in the process of trying to solve the problem when Grover Mills appeared. He came down from working on the new room and into the kitchen, where he helped himself to a doughnut and cup of coffee. My solution was standing only two feet away from me.

"Grover," I said, "isn't that Nima some guy?"

"Yup," he said as he reached in the cupboard for the sugar bowl. "I got him loading the pickup right now for a trip to the dump."

"I don't think I've ever seen Nima take to anyone as he's taken to you," I said.

I wasn't sure that Grover had heard the compliment because he began telling me something about the price of Vermont weatherboard. I tried again.

"Seems as if you're all Nima talks about anymore. How he enjoys being with you and all."

Finally Grover responded. "Yup, he's a heck of a kid." Then he looked inside the refrigerator and added, "You know we've been out of cream now for the last three days."

*Kerrie, Geoffrey, and Grover Mills at their farm in Connecticut, where Nima stayed while we were in Europe. Grover became Nima's hero, and Geoffrey Nima's.*

There were times I got the distinct feeling that because Grover built our kitchen he felt he was entitled to some sort of a 99-year lease on the refrigerator. But that didn't bother me now. In fact, I felt that feeding Grover was a small price to pay for what I was about to ask.

Even before I explained the entire situation, Grover said, "No problem." I told Grover that he had first better check with his wife, Kerrie, to make sure that it was okay. But on the chance that he would forget, I phoned her myself that evening.

Kerrie said that Grover *had* told them at dinner and that they were all looking forward to it, especially their six-year-old son, Geoffrey. She said that Geoffrey was already planning all the things they were going to do with Nima. The first weekend Nima arrived they would go to the local fair, the Peking Chinese Restaurant in Westport, and horseback riding.

Knowing that Nima would be staying with Grover, Kerrie, and Geoffrey, we could leave for England assured that he would be safe and sound. They lived on a small farm in Easton, about eight miles from us, where they had chickens, turkeys, a cow, a horse, a pony, and a dog. Nima would feel more at home there than with us. During the day Nima would still work with Grover, and on weekends he would help out on the farm. Grover even offered to drive Nima to school two nights a week so that he wouldn't get behind in his lessons. Nima had been doing very well in class, and he looked forward to those evenings.

Before I hung up with Kerrie, I had warned her that Nima was not really used to electrical appliances. But after I said that, I realized it wasn't necessary. They both understood cultural differences from their two-year stint in the Peace Corps.

I was going to tell Kerrie about the time Nima almost burnt our house down stoking the electric oven with firewood, but I decided against it. It would only put an unnecessary burden of worry on her while she was at work. However, I did mention that Nima had gotten lost on his bike more than once. Kerrie seemed surprised to hear that a Sherpa guide could actually get lost. They were supposed to have a nose for direction.

In the last few weeks we had received regular phone calls from in and around Westport. Nima would be on the other end. His story was always the same, the location was always different.

"Daily best wishes. Nima here." He would begin each phone call with the formality of a British lord.

"Nima ride bikes many hour, many mile. Nima see many good peoples, many good house, many good store."

Then there would be a long pause.

"Nima very sorry. Nima no know how take bikes back home. Next time Nima no get lost."

Then Nima would hand over the phone to the people at the house where he had stopped so that they could give us directions to pick him up. The first few times Nima got lost and we picked him up, he felt very sheepish. But he soon got used to it and so did we. The last two times he came running out of the house, waved a friendly hand to the people in the doorway, dumped the bike in the trunk, hopped in the back seat, and filled us in on the wonderful ride he had had, the wonderful new people he had met and the fantastic place he had stopped for ice cream.

Although Nima's new camaraderie with Grover seemed to have helped him adjust to many of the perils of Western life, it hadn't helped him to become more independent of John and me. He still never liked to be left at home—especially at night. Almost always Nima went wherever we went. But there had been a few occasions where John and I wanted to have an evening out alone. One of those times was now. It was our anniversary. I went into Nima's room and explained that John and I were going out to celebrate our four-year marriage. Then I told Nima to follow me into the kitchen so I could show him that his dinner was in the oven, staying warm with the switch off. In light of that firewood-in-the-oven incident, I reminded him more than once not to touch any of the dials. I was just about to hand him a slip of paper with the restaurant's phone number in case of an emergency when I noticed the look on his face.

"Nima no go?" he said.

"Not this time, Nima." I tried to explain that anniversaries were not like birthday parties, but I wasn't so sure Nima understood.

"Memsahib, Sahib go out in *cars?*"

"Yes, Nima, but not far. Just here in Westport."

Nima nodded. Then he peeked in the oven at his frozen dinner and said, "Memsahib and Sahib eat good dinners. No worry about Nima."

John was standing next to me. I wasn't sure what was going through his head, but I was thinking that we were the two biggest rats who had ever crawled the earth.

After John went through the house turning on all the outside lights and checking to make sure all the doors were locked, we got into the car. It seemed so strange to us that Nima was scared to stay home alone. He had lived a life so dangerous I got the chills just thinking about it. When we were in the car, John started the engine but then turned off the ignition. He went back into the house and told Nima to grab his jacket, that we were all going to Dameon's for dinner. Our anniversary would be a convivial threesome instead of an intimate twosome.

There are two restaurants in Westport that are always jumping: Mario's and Dameon's. One main reason is that they are directly across the street from the Westport railroad station. The 7:05'ers who get off the cattle car have only a thirty-second jog to either establishment before they stabilize themselves for their 2.2 kids, electronic computer games, and leaking Jacuzzi faucets.

Nima preferred the subtle European cuisine at Dameon's over Mario's homespun Italian food. He also liked listening to the jazz pianist as he ate his vegetarian ratatouille and eyed the characters who floated in and out.

The night of our anniversary dinner, we were seated at a window table. I was telling Nima what the Millses had planned for his stay. Nima seemed excited about everything, except the horseback riding. He didn't understand why anyone would want to ride aimlessly in the woods when you could get into a car and go shopping in Westport.

After our drinks came, Nima began counting all the station wagons that were lined up waiting for the 7:05 out of Grand Central. Suddenly a limousine the size of a hearse double-parked in front of our window. Out poured an Arab sheik toting a Gucci attaché case. Behind him was his entourage. The group, who looked as if they were preparing for a U.N. meeting, were shown to a table next to ours.

Before they even had a chance to order their dinner, two policemen came in and spoke to the sheik. John and I couldn't hear over the music, but Nima said that the cops had asked to see his papers, and the sheik had told the cops to go out and talk to his chauffeur. Since Nima, John, and I were seated at a window, we had a perfect view of the outside transaction between the two policemen and the limousine driver.

Unfortunately, our entertainment was short-lived. Everything must have been on the up-and-up, because after the chauffeur showed the policemen a wad of papers, they returned to their squad cars. As we watched them drive away, Nima told us that he thought the reason the police came in was because the guy with the towel on his head didn't look like the rest of us.

Later I thought more about what Nima said. That statement was a clear indication that Nima could be losing his Sherpa identity, and worse, taking on ours. If, after just two months, Nima began to lose touch with who he was, what would he do after six months? I was almost afraid to speculate.

That night before we went to bed, John said that he was seriously beginning to wonder if the longer Nima stayed, the harder it would be for him when he returned to the

Himalayas. As it was now, there wasn't anything Nima didn't admire about the United States.

Perhaps John was right. Nima's visit to America could make it difficult for him to go back home to the high mountains. Nima was getting used to our Western comforts—too used to them. Just days earlier, John mentioned to Nima that it might be fun for us to pack a lunch and go hiking in a nearby nature preserve. In so many words, Nima said that he didn't see the point. He suggested that we get into the car and drive around. This was clearly not the Nima we had known back in the Himalayas.

There, he had had boundless energy. We had first really noticed it on the seventh day of our trek, in a village called Jiri. Besides fetching the wood for the campfire and hauling the water for dinner, he insisted on doing all our laundry himself, even though Mingma instructed Pasang to share the workload.

After a full day spent down at the river banging our clothes against rocks, then drying them in the hot midday sun, he returned with the clothes neatly folded, as if from a professional laundry. For all his effort, he would not accept any rupees, just chocolate bars, which he immediately broke into tiny pieces to share with Mingma, Pasang, and all the porters. This habit would continue throughout the entire trek. Whenever John and I pleaded with Nima to take some money for whatever job he did, he would refuse, claiming that he enjoyed the physical work—if he didn't work he would go crazy.

Each day after lunch, John and I would lay against our back packs and watch Nima and Pasang clean up the pots and pans. They went at it with a vigor I had never seen before. They polished the battered metalware until it sparkled. But they used no soap; they cleaned with mud, grass, and ashes from the fire.

*Compared to most of the others we had to cross, this swinging bridge was very sophisticated. It spanned a deep chasm.*

Each evening around the fire, the porters would squat and sing, enjoying their rest after having hauled sixty-pound loads up and down the slopes. Shim, our favorite porter, would roll cigarettes for them with great skill, using a rough, stemmy local tobacco and dried rhododendron leaves for the wrapper. The smoke was sour, but the cigarettes were rolled at every rest stop, and the porters seemed to suck them in so deeply it was no wonder they all had hacking coughs. Mingma and Pasang, more elegant, used snuff. Nima used neither—something he constantly reminded us of.

The Sherpas' and porters' enjoyment of a life with little material comfort amazed me. Western materialism seemed unable to provide such a simple sense of exuberance. The more material comforts we gained, the less satisfied we seemed to get. Maybe a good part of the meaning of truth lay in this uncomplicated satisfaction with the simple life.

But while admiring this joy of life, I had been suffering the lack of Western amenities. There was no way I could carry even a ten-pound load up those torturous trails in bare feet, and then burst into song around the campfire as the porters did. Even if I wanted to, I could not change places with them. I felt false and uncomfortable, as if I were an intruder. We had been struggling up and down those peaks and valley to try to get some glimmer of ultimate truth, and by Day Eight we had made no progress whatever toward our goal.

The book John had intended to write was not materializing. The monks and lamas we had been interviewing seemed unable to offer any fresh insights. The physical demands of the trek commanded all of our attention. It was hard for us to tell where we were headed. We had lost focus. There's an old saying that John kept repeating: "They change their skies but not their hearts, those who sail away." Maybe that summed up our situation.

Perhaps days later, when in sight of the great Himalayan range, near the high monasteries, that would change. But when we left Jiri the next morning on Day Nine, I had to admit to a dull sense of fear.

We got into camp early on Day Nine, at three in the afternoon. We were moving into Sherpa country, and the architecture of the houses began to show it. On the first floor was a dark, straw-covered room with hay for the sheep and goats. A rough-hewn stairway led to the main room—usually combined living, sleeping, and dining quarters. All the homes resembled Nima's, although we were still days away from meeting his family far up in the Solu Khumbu.

I had been wondering how Mingma picked out the camping sites each night, but not until this day did I find out. Mingma knew practically every possible site from his many treks. A river or stream was essential. With that taken care of, he would simply go to the village headman or farm owner and ask permission, giving him a few rupees as he did so. In return, the Sherpas were scrupulous in cleaning up the campsite the following morning. It was always left cleaner than when we arrived.

Early on the morning of Day Ten, we got ready to attack the Changma Pass. John reminded me that it was three Empire State Buildings above us. It would, however, lead us deeper into the Sherpa country, where the ambiance and topography of the real Himalayas would become more profound.

Across from the campfire, the porters were in the mess tent, huddled together to take advantage of each other's warmth. They had slept a little late, and Mingma had sent Nima to wake them. He did it mischievously by releasing the main tent rope, tumbling the canvas down on them in a single swift motion. The porters untangled themselves, roaring with laughter, while Shim, the youngest porter, chased Nima halfway up a hill for vengeance. By that time, they were too tired for a wrestling match, and they walked back down arm in arm to pack up the camp.

Climbing toward the Changma Pass, a thin and pale village woman was being carried on the back of her husband toward Jiri, where there was a small clinic. She winced at every step her husband took, as he moved down the steep rocky trail toward us. It seemed a miracle that he didn't

*One of the many* mani *walls we encountered along the trail. The slabs of stone are covered with the prayer* Øm mani padme hum *(the jewel in the eye of the lotus).*

stumble and send both of them over the side of the narrow path. It would be another day, perhaps two, before they would reach Jiri. We would never know if they reached it in time.

Three days earlier we had passed a similar sight: a boy of fourteen, obviously in pain, being carried in a straw chair on the back of a porter, facing backward, an umbrella over his head to block the sun. Behind him, his father walked, arms folded across his chest, mumbling a prayer. But he took time to say namaste to us as he continued on the trail.

When we reached the top of the Changma Pass, we could tell we were in the Buddhist territory. At the pass was one of the largest collections of *mani* walls in Nepal. There intricately carved prayer stones—considerably bulkier than the rosary beads Nima would later compare them to in the hospital—stretched along the trail for scores of yards. We dutifully walked to the left of them, just as Bobby Chettri had instructed us to do. About shoulder-high, the slabs of smooth stone were imbedded in the walls. They were gracefully carved in Tibetan script. The words that had been laboriously chiseled into the stones, repeat over and over again: *Om mani padme hum*. Translated, this basic Buddhist invocation means "the jewel in the eye of the lotus" literally, but it is full of symbolic significance for the enlightened. The phrase symbolizes the self, the Buddha, and the universe and its immutable laws.

I wondered why so much effort and artistry had been expended on these lonely, wind-blown slopes and passes. In many parts of the world, these prayer stones would be considered useless billboards to the gods. But here they belonged. The long stretches of stone prayers burst with devotion, love, and compassion.

Each man who inscribes a stone gains merit, the ultimate goal in the Sherpa religion. This is *the* priority, the tacit admission that what happens after death is more important than what happened in this life. The prayer walls reflect a tribute to the belief that this life is an illusion, that the arduous labor to create the walls is a selfless act to neutralize selfish craving, the cause of all unhappiness according to Buddha.

We paused at the path, resting and looking out over the

*A prayer wall being meticulously carved along the trail. The artisans receive no money for their efforts—just full reward in their next life.*

endless trail ahead. The snow-covered peaks were still hiding from us, except for Gauri Shankar in the distance, once thought to be the highest mountain in the world. Surrounding us were white prayer flags fluttering in the breeze. They were thin, gauzy, and printed with invocations; the belief is that as they flutter, the prayers are sent out over the earth by the winds.

The pass at Changma was only a warm-up for the Lamjura Pass, which we prepared to tackle the following day. It was the highest we were to cross on the long way to Everest. At our campsite, in a village called Kenja, the range loomed above us. It looked cold, snow covered, and forbidding. The feeling was intensified when the older porter in threadbare clothes bowed to us as we were eating our porridge, said the usual namaste, then pointed toward the high ridge. Nima came over to explain that the old man and two other porters did not feel they could surmount the pass with their loads. Two new porters from the village had been hired to replace them. The food supplies were being gradually consumed, so the loads were getting lighter to the extent that more porters would be dropped to return to Kathmandu as we continued on the trail.

We somehow struggled up through another forest of firs and rhododendrons, sprinkled with gentian and oak. By eleven we had reached the little village of Sete, where a beautiful rectangular monument with four pairs of eyes of Buddha looked out severely in all directions. Nearby was a small temple, which we entered with Nima, Pasang, and Mingma. With reverence, all three dropped to their knees, bowed, and touched their foreheads to the floor.

Their gesture was moving. Up to this point, their religion had been reflected in their actions: their basic sense of cheerfulness, their eagerness to be helpful, their respect for us and for themselves, their warmth, kindness, and sense of humor (except of course, when Mingma's Napoleonic complex got the better of him).

The Sherpas firmly believe in life after death. The strength of this belief governs nearly every action of their lives. They believe that there are immutable laws of the universe that are only mildly reflected by various gods they inherited from more primitive times. Their ancestors had come over from Tibet with a mixture of Tantric Buddhism and the primitive ritual of *Bon,* with various gods and demons that remain as vestigial remnants of their roots.

More important to the Sherpas is the moral order that they try to observe in their everyday living, their relations with their fellow human beings. Since they believe that every action, small or large, will be rewarded or punished after death, this means that the material world comes second in importance to the moral world. What counts is the exact and almost computerized balance of good and bad actions of this temporal life. Every act adds to the score. Hardship and material gain mean little or nothing, the gaining of merit everything. Merit comes from kindness, honesty, devotion, and love for humanity. Gaining merit does not guarantee worldly success; it means only reward in the life beyond.

The memory of Nima, Pasang, and Mingma prostrating themselves on the temple floor in reverence to Buddha made me realize the importance of Nima maintaining his spiritual identity in the wilds of Connecticut. Perhaps Nima was now becoming too involved with our Western ways because of his sudden withdrawal from a very structured way of life. I blamed myself for that. When he was in the hospital I had promised Nima that, as soon as he was well enough, we would visit a Jewish temple. It was now two and a half months later, and we had never made that visit. Although John and I were busy getting ready to leave for England, I vowed that I would somehow make the time to take Nima to that temple.

Unfortunately, now that Nima was well again, he didn't seem at all interested in going to a temple. I asked him if he would prefer going to a Catholic church, perhaps talking to a priest, or maybe just going to the church and meditating. Nima said that if he went anywhere, he would like it to be the Jewish temple. He felt certain that that would be the closest thing to his own place of worship.

The evening Nima and I set out for the temple turned out to be the same evening that the rabbi was running through a bar mitzvah rehearsal. In fact, the rabbi was walking through the temple doors at the same time we were. We all nodded. Then I realized that we might be intruding. I stopped the rabbi, who was a few steps ahead of us, and as briefly as I could, I explained the situation.

All during my explanation, the rabbi looked from Nima to me with a half smile and slight twinkle in his eye, almost as if he thought we might be putting him on. But after I finished what turned out to be quite a lengthy explanation, he turned to Nima and said, "Nima, I'm quite flattered that of all the religious institutions, you have chosen a temple."

Nima bowed his head and silently performed the namaste salutation. "I very happy to visit temple," he said. Then Nima took a quick glance around the vestibule and added, "It is a good and strong temple."

"You have lamas in your Buddhist temples—is that right?" the rabbi asked.

Nima didn't answer right away. His eyes were still darting around the temple, as if he were preparing to give an estimate on repairs. Finally Nima said, "Many lamas. Many temples."

I began telling the rabbi how involved the selection process for a new reincarnate lama was. The Buddhist claimed that the method brought direct evidence that the child selected was indeed the reincarnation of a lama who had recently died. With the aid of mediums, they would seek the probable location of the child they were looking for. Once found, the child would be the object of intense study by the monks of the monastery. He would be asked what he remembered about his former life and the monastery from which he purportedly came.

If the child was successful in supplying clear and unassailable information in this regard, he would be placed in front of the former lama's clothes and possessions. These were intentionally intermixed with other such material. If he selected unerringly the proper articles and discarded the others, he would then be declared the true incarnate lama. Whether he was two or five or ten years old, he would be brought to the monastery and trained in its traditions to serve as a future lama.

The rabbi was listening attentively. Then he said, "You must have many temples near your home, Nima."

"Sherpas have many temples for praying and for festival times," Nima said. He began telling the rabbi how Sherpas gather for various holidays, and how some will walk for days to take part in the temple's festivities. Then he got specific. He described the Mani-Rimdu festival, at which Sherpas from all over the Solu Khumbu gather at Teng-boche Monastery, not only to gain merit in the next life but to enjoy themselves by watching the lamas and monks dance in the courtyard and perform acts of good over evil. At the last Mani-Rimdu, he said, Mingma showed up drunk with two Sherpas. He gave only ten rupees and no chicken. Before Nima could elaborate further, I said that we had taken up enough of the rabbi's time, even though the rabbi didn't appear to be in a great hurry.

Finally, after Nima told us a bit more about how cheap and disrespectful Mingma was at festival time, he reached into his wallet, retrieved two dollars, and passed them to the rabbi in one hand, as he did his "take it easy" handshake with the other.

The rabbi seemed so surprised by the two bucks Nima slammed in his hand that he immediately turned to me for an explanation. After I told him how no Sherpa would ever go into a temple without giving a donation to either the lama or the monk, the rabbi nodded, thanked Nima and told him that the money would go for the world hunger program. Then he invited Nima and me to come inside. If we wanted to, we could watch the run-through of the bar mitzvah. The last thing the rabbi said to Nima was to feel free to come by anytime to pray or just to chat. The last thing Nima said to the rabbi was, "Take it easy, ya hear."

Nima and I took a seat at the back of the temple. The moment we got settled, Nima reached into his jean jacket and fished out a crumpled red bandana. I thought for a brief second that he was going to put it around his neck. But I wasn't even close. He carefully opened it and inside were the rosary beads that the priest had given him back in the hospital. My initial reaction was to nudge him to put them away—we were in a temple. But that first instinct was based on my own hang-ups from Catholic school. For years the nuns had warned us that if we had ever dared to step our little pagan bodies inside another place of worship, God would turn us into Communists. By the time I was ten I was a Communist twenty-eight times over.

After about twenty minutes of watching Nima spin each glass bead as if he had been doing it his whole life, he put them away. Then we both watched the rabbi instructing two twelve-year-old boys for another ten minutes.

On the way home, Nima seemed surprised that the Jewish temple didn't smell of yak-butter candles. And that there were no statues of Lord Buddha. In fact there wasn't even one picture of him. However, he did say that he liked the rabbi. And he intended to take him up on his offer to drop by sometime and say, "How's it going?"

The day before John and I left for England, I promised Nima that I'd help him get his things ready to take to Grover's. But when I went into his room with the blow dryer I was lending him, I was stunned. The place looked as if he were going on a three-year world tour, not a two-week stay eight miles away. Spread neatly from one corner of his room to the other were jeans, T-shirts, sweaters, and shoes. Along the length of his dresser were his bathrobe, pajamas, and slippers. And on the sofa was a large plastic bag that I took to be filled with scraps of paper: they turned out to be coupons. He said that he didn't want to just leave them lying around in an empty house. Next to the coupons was another bag filled with gifts: a package of Hostess Ding Dongs for Grover, a box of Morton salt for Kerrie (salt in the Himalayas is as precious as gold is here), and a bag of Bubble Yum for Geoffrey. In his bathroom the medicine chest was empty. All the toilet articles, including those three tubes of toothpaste, were spilling out of John's old shaving kit.

Nima asked me if I thought he had forgotten anything. I told him that from one quick glance it looked as if everything were there. Then I suggested he hurry up and get it all packed—we had things to do. Late that afternoon Nima and I went into Westport for some last-minute purchases. I picked up a pair of comfortable walking shoes for the streets of London, and Nima picked up workman's boots. Ever since he had been working with Grover and his carpenters, that was all he talked about buying.

He now had several hundred dollars stashed away, and thirty of those were set aside for boots. However, the day we went shopping I made a deal with Nima. I told him that I thought it would be fair if he saved his money for the teahouse and I bought him the boots. He could work off the price of the boots by doing extra chores around the house.

As it was, Nima had refused to take any money for helping me clean the house ever since he had begun working with Grover. He said that we were the same as his parents and he would never take money from them. And besides that, we had already done too much for him. Now, Nima wore the boots into the house with a whole new spring to his step. As soon as he got into the living room, he took off one boot and inspected it both inside and out. Then he turned to me and said that the boots were worth a lot more than just extra chores around the house. They were worth the chores, he said, plus a surprise gift, which he would personally build. When I heard the word *build* my mind flashed to all sorts of things—all of them potential disasters. In recent weeks, Nima had mentioned more than once how practical a barn would be in our backyard. He said that way John could have fresh meat every night. And I wouldn't have to be running to Peter's for milk and cheese. In addition to the barn, he also commented that there didn't seem to be any teahouses in Fairfield County.

I suddenly had visions of coming back from England and finding a Sherpa teahouse down by the river, or a barn loaded with animals outside our bedroom window. But after I gave those possibilities some thought, I realized I was letting my imagination get the better of me. However, the day we left for England I casually mentioned to Nima that I was glad John and I had never built a barn or teahouse on our property.

# EIGHT

THROUGHOUT OUR WEEK in England we kept thinking and wondering what Nima was up to. All Nima ever talked about from the time he had first met Grover was Grover. I learned more about Grover than I cared to know. At dinner, Nima would tell us everything from Grover's not liking mustard on his bagel, to Grover's net worth and daily bank deposit, to how Grover was always clowning around with waitresses. In fact, Nima did more than just talk about Grover, he began to dress like him as well. Grover had given Nima an old tool-belt equipped with what Nima said was a True Temper rocket hammer, a Stanley "Life Guard yellow" ruler, a number-six Phillips Head screwdriver, and a Miller's Falls utility knife. Nima wore that thing as if it were a life-support system. The only time he took it off was when he went to bed or we were going out for the evening. A couple of times he wore the belt to class. But that soon stopped. Nima said that one of the teachers from another class had asked him to fix a broken light switch, thinking he was an electrician.

In addition to dressing like Grover, and combing his hair off to the side, as Grover did, he also talked like him, affecting some kind of a strange New England twang. He also replaced, or at least he tried to replace, his short, bouncy step with the slower, more methodical swagger that characterized Grover. The two of them together were quite a pair. When Grover hopped into the pickup, Nima hopped in right next to him and rode shotgun along the Fairfield County roads.

The day we arrived home from England it was pouring rain. I wondered if Grover and Nima would be working indoors or out. Nima didn't like it when it rained. But I thought that was mostly because Grover didn't like it when it rained. The minute we cleared customs, I phoned the Millses. Kerrie answered. She told me that Nima had been a perfect house guest. He not only helped with most of the meals, but he constantly picked up after everyone. Kerrie said she felt like a real slob at first, but I explained how Nima did the same thing for John and me. He was appallingly fastidious. She also said that Nima and Geoffrey had become inseparable. Just as Nima had been one pace behind Grover, so Geoffrey followed Nima everywhere. Nima watched over Geoffrey as if he were his little brother.

Then Kerrie laughed and said that the only thing Nima wouldn't do was milk Holly. But Nima had politely explained to Kerrie that milking cows or naks (a female yak) is woman's work. No male Sherpa would milk a nak, unless he happened to be a Khamba.

Kerrie asked, half seriously, if we were sure we wanted Nima back. She said they were all going to miss having him around, especially listening to his dinnertime stories. Nima had entertained them with tales of Phakding, his near escapes from dangerous ice-falls, his years at the Hillary school, and a year-by-year chronology of how he astutely worked his way up from porter to Mountain Travel guide.

Then Kerrie asked me, in a puzzled voice, "What's with

some character called Mingma?" I was about to fill Kerrie in on Mingma, but John had found a porter, and he was signaling me to hurry. Before I hung up, Kerrie said that Grover, Nima, and Geoffrey would all be at our house when we got there.

The second I stepped foot in the house, I sensed something was up. Geoffrey bounded out of the kitchen toward John and me, clutching a half-devoured peanut butter sandwich, as Nima and Grover, without even a hello, ducked out the front door. Then Geoffrey wrapped his sticky fingers around my wrist and ordered us to follow him into Nima's room. He leaped on top of Nima's sleeper sofa and pedaled his muddy little Adidases from one end to the other, trying to close the shutters. John and I were instructed not to ask any questions concerning our captivity. The only information he volunteered was that Nima taught him to count to ten in Sherpa. By the time he had demonstrated his knowledge of Pidgin Sherpa, two or three times, we heard Grover and Nima return.

Nima called out, "Okay, Geoffrey." That was apparently Geoffrey's cue to release us. He led us into the living room with strict instructions not to open our eyes until told otherwise.

"Okay, Memsahib, Sahib, open eye," Nima said.

Standing between Nima and Grover was a newly built bookcase, a bookcase handmade by Nima. Grover quickly told us that the only help he gave Nima was in supplying the tools, scraps of lumber, and the use of his workshop. The actual carpentry had been done by Nima himself, after work, before work, and on the weekend. The only person prouder than Grover was Nima. Nima pointed out his meticulously drawn pencil lines, his perfectly symmetrical supporting dividers, and the almost flawless pine.

*Nima putting the finishing touches on the bookcase he made for me in Grover's workshop.*

Nima's handcrafted bookcase was without doubt one of the most special gifts I had ever received. It was also one of the strangest bookcases I had ever seen. The only books that would fit into the cubbyholes were offsize paperbacks and extremely small hardcovers. But that didn't matter. It was the idea that Nima had spent countless hours to build something he knew I had wanted and needed. Weeks before, Nima had come with me to the Sloane's furniture store in Westport to check out the prices on their bookshelves. When the salesman showed us to the corner of the store where they had bookcases, Nima lost no time giving them the Grover once-over. He inspected them from all angles, carefully checking to see how they were put together. He even measured the thickness of the shelves with the Stanley Life Guard Yellow ruler that was hanging on his tool belt. Then Nima asked, "How much?" The salesman told us $250, including brackets. Nima had gotten used to being quoted high prices, but he hadn't gotten the hang of how to say politely, "Well, we're just looking today," and then walk away.

Nima told the salesman, who was a gray-haired, friendly enough gentleman, that he was a carpenter for the Grover Mills Construction Company. Nima enunciated "Grover Mills" the same way a preppy drags out the name of his country club. The salesman didn't appear to be overly impressed. Then Nima leaned back against a teakwood dining room table on display, crossed one leg, dug a thumb inside his tool belt, and told the salesman that Grover pays his best carpenter, Mike, ten big ones an hour. The salesman's mouth dropped. Nima told him that he and Grover dealt *directly* with Fairfield Lumber and that he could get number-two pine for a buck per board-foot, and that a set of bookshelves just like these would take roughly eighteen to twenty board-feet. Then Nima jerked his Fairfield Lumber baseball cap to prove that he really did have connections. Nima quickly figured that the bookshelves could be made for forty dollars. When the salesman turned his back, probably looking for the concealed Candid Camera, Nima whispered that I should offer him no more than forty.

I whispered back that I really didn't care for those shelves, and that we should look somewhere else. Nima agreed. On the way home he said that Grover wouldn't have given him a bagel and an egg for the sloppy shelves.

Now, on our first day back from England, I was face to face with those bookshelves and what Nima reminded me was a $250 saving. After we got through raving to Nima about his brilliant work, he went into his bedroom and came out with the Polaroid. Nima didn't even give us a chance to take off our coats. He immediately positioned me on one side of the bookcase and John on the other. Then he handed the camera to Grover and asked him if he'd mind taking a picture. But before Grover did so, Nima grabbed his True Temper Rocket hammer off his belt and pretended to be hammering the side of the bookcase. When the photo came out, Nima let us each have a quick look before he took the picture back into his room. He said that it would be enclosed in his next letter to Mingma.

Later that evening, after Geoffrey and Grover had left, Nima filled us in on the details of his stay. He told us about the helicopter ride they took, and how it set Grover back twenty-five big ones for only fifteen minutes. Nima said that Grover, Kerrie, and Geoffrey had never been on one before, whereas he had flown one seven times between Lukla airstrip and Kathmandu. Nima said he wasn't that keen to get on a small helicopter in Danbury, when he had been used to buzzing the roof of the world with mountain expeditions. But he did go, if only to hold Geoffrey's hand.

Nima also told us about the great dinner they had at a

Chinese restaurant, and how a *foreign* waiter from Canton kept asking him a million different questions about his mountain-climbing experiences. Knowing Nima, I was curious about how much the waiter actually asked and how much Nima gratuitously offered.

Then Nima described in detail an incident of the previous week.

"Grover drop Nima off lumberyard," Nima began. "Grover say, 'See Ray in pine shed. Ask for special order—fifteen light French door.' Nima go pine shed, say, 'How's it going?' to Ray. Ray say door no here. Fred have door in shop.

"Nima go shop say, 'How's it going?' to Fred. Fred say door no here. Door with Ray in pine shed. Nima go back to pine shed say, "'How's it going?' again to Ray. Ray say go office. Nima go office. Office boss say, 'I got Grover door.' Nima say good. Boss man say Ray have door. Nima say Ray *no* have door. Boss man say Ray *have* door. Nima go back see Ray. No Ray. Stubby in pine shed. Nima say, 'How's it going?' to Stubby. Stubby say see Ray. Ray in trailer. Nima go trailer but see Grover. Grover get mad. Grover and Nima get in pick-up go for bagel and egg at deli. Next day Ray call and say found door in other building."

Nima continued to fill us in on other jobs he and Grover went on, the places they stopped for lunch, and the ridiculous cost of building materials. Nima was beginning to sound more like Grover every day. Everything that poured from Grover's lips eventually worked its way to Nima's mouth.

While Nima was helping me load the dishes in the dishwasher, he began telling me about his English teacher at Staples. Nima said that Mr. Mastroberadino told him he had an uncanny knack for picking up the English language, and that the other students, even the ones who were here permanently, did not have his ability. Then Nima asked me if I remembered the very short girl in his class who was here from Thailand, the girl we had run into down at Westport Pizza the day Joe accidentally put sausage on the pizza instead of an extra layer of cheese. I told Nima I vaguely remembered her.

As Nima wiped down the butcher-block top, he told me he had been talking to the girl during a school coffee break. She had told him she was staying here permanently, not going back to her country. Nima asked me what kind of papers she had to be able to stay here forever. I explained to him about visas, and how his visa was good for only six months. Nima just looked at me and nodded. It didn't take much to realize what this was all leading to.

After he made himself a triple-scoop ice-cream cone, he asked me if I thought it was a good idea for someone who didn't speak as well as she did to stay here forever. I told Nima that I couldn't make a value judgment, since I didn't know all the circumstances. But Nima seemed to know the circumstances. He told me that the girl said she was very happy to stay here; that it was heaven for her. She said her home in Thailand was very poor with "no-good house, no-good foods, no-good peoples." She loved America because all people here were good. The girl planned to send money to her mother, father, brothers, and sisters. One day she would go back and visit them. She had many friends in this country and a family she was living with who, Nima said, was "the same like her mother and same like her father, and she loved them same like her own mother and father. And the family said that she was same like son." When Nima said "same like son," I realized the seriousness of our situation. All of our fears that Nima might never want to go home seemed to be coming true.

The next morning, before I even got out of bed, I reviewed exactly what I would say to him. I would lay it on the line. I would explain that although we loved him just like a son, it was for his own good that he go back to the Himalayas. I had also prepared some clear-cut examples to demonstrate graphically that America is not everything Nima had it cracked up to be. I'd tell him about crime, inner cities, unemployment, hospital costs, inflation, and interest rates.

I was in the process of making Nima's and John's favorite breakfast—waffles—when Nima came into the kitchen. He must have heard the Cuisinart and figured it was either waffles or pancakes. As he came in, I swallowed hard and hoped that I could get the right words out in the right order.

"How's it goin', Memsahib?"

"Not bad. What do you want, blueberry or apple?"

"Memsahib like blueberry?"

"Love it. Blueberry it is." While I was defrosting the frozen blueberries, Nima sat on the barstool and told me how you bevel a plank. I couldn't concentrate on Nima's shoptalk, I was so absorbed in working out what I was going to say to him. As soon as Nima stopped to take a breath, I would cut in. But Nima didn't seem to need air. He went right from how you use a block plane for smoothing off the edge of a board to how he *couldn't wait* to go back to Phakding and build the best teahouse the Solu Khumbu had ever seen.

I caught my breath. Go *back* to Phakding? Build his teahouse? Looking forward to it? Suddenly, a great pressure was lifted from me. All my worries were gone.

But then, just as suddenly, I was *hurt*. Nima didn't have to be *that* enthusiastic about going back. Hadn't he considered how John and I felt? Didn't he know how much we loved him? Didn't he appreciate everything we had done for him? Didn't he know how much we were going to miss him after he left? It was no longer necessary for me to tell Nima all the ugly things about America—he obviously knew them.

With the Thanksgiving holiday coming up, John was looking forward to picking up Judd, his eighteen-year-old son, from college. He was, however, a little apprehensive about any hidden jealousy that might be simmering within Judd. John based this fear on that fact that twice we had had to disappoint Judd and miss football games because Nima was too weak to make the trip. Besides that, Nima had almost become a surrogate son. John felt that there might have developed a sort of sibling rivalry, at least on a subconscious level.

About ten minutes after John left to pick up Judd, Nima came out of his bedroom dressed for work. While he was breaking eggs for an omelet, he asked if John ever got mad at Judd for going outside without his jacket on, or riding the bike on the Weston roads after four in the afternoon. I told Nima that I didn't remember Judd doing those specific things, but that John got just as angry when Judd blasted the stereo. Nima dropped his English muffins into the toaster and asked how many years of schooling Judd had had. I told him that he was beginning his thirteenth year. (I didn't want to get into an involved explanation about kindergarten or nursery school.) As I was heading out of the kitchen, Nima asked if Judd knew how to install a zero-clearance fireplace. I told Nima that I doubted it. Nima said that he would teach him how, and that maybe Judd could go on a job with Grover and him and say, "How's it going?" to the guys down at Fairfield Lumber. They could even stop at the deli for a bagel and egg. I told Nima that that sounded like a good idea.

Minutes later, I was in my office when there was a light knock on the door. It was Nima. He wanted to know if we had any pictures of Judd. I went into John's office and dug out Judd's senior high school picture. Nima studied the three-by-five from all angles before returning it. Then he said that Judd and he looked a lot alike. They both had the same eyes, hair, and teeth. Although I couldn't detect any physical similarities, I didn't tell Nima that. Instead, I pointed out that they were both eighteen, both very bright, and both had a good sense of humor. Nima seemed to agree.

Shortly after one o'clock, John and Judd pulled into the driveway. Nima was home. He had only worked half a day because the Millses were taking a long Thanksgiving weekend. I called into Nima's room, where he was probably either washing up or counting his money.

Just as Judd came through the door, Nima appeared. He was freshly showered, with his hair slicked to the side like Grover's; he wore painter pants and a T-shirt that said Mills Construction Company; casually slung over his linguine-thin hips was his tool belt.

John made the introductions. Nima and Judd were both disgustingly polite. It was like when Exxon meets Mobil. I was glad that the lunch was ready and we didn't have to stand around listening to any more of this.

During lunch Judd asked Nima a few polite questions about his country. Nima asked Judd a few polite questions about his college. John and I, picking up on the wind-chill factor, carefully split our questions down the center. For every question directed at Judd, one was directed at Nima.

As soon as we finished eating, Nima jumped up and

began clearing the table. Judd got up to help, but Nima told Judd to sit and talk to his "real father." I got up to help Nima, while Judd and John talked about fraternities and rush week. Finally, Judd went out to the car and brought in his notebook and started showing John a few of the articles that he had written for the college newspaper.

After the kitchen was cleaned up, Nima disappeared into his room. Seconds later he came out with *his* notebook from his English class. Nima took a seat at the other end of the room and appeared to be doing his homework. It was the first time I had ever seen Nima get out his homework voluntarily. After a few minutes, Nima got up, went over to John, and asked him if he could give him some sentences using the verb "to be." Nima had never before asked John for help with his homework. He always asked me to go over his papers with him.

John put down Judd's articles and picked up Nima's notebook. Just as I had expected, Judd didn't appear to be overly thrilled that Nima had usurped his time with his father. Judd was all set to get up, when John asked Judd if he could think of a sentence using the verb "to be." Judd thought for about a second and came up with a sentence. Nima told Judd that that was a very good sentence. And that's what finally broke the cold spell. Judd gave Nima about five more sentences, and Nima gave Judd one sloppy compliment after the other on his good sentences. Soon they were going through each other's notebooks. Judd was showing Nima an article that he had written, and Nima was showing Judd a letter he had written in Sanskrit to his mother. Judd said that he could never do as well with Sanskrit characters as Nima was doing in English. Nima told Judd that he, Nima, could never write for a newspaper.

It wasn't much later that I heard Judd on the phone,

telling his friend David that he had a good friend here from the Himalayas whom he wanted him to meet. He reassured David that Nima was a "real cool dude." Nima was sitting on the barstool next to the phone, beaming.

Before Judd hung up, their plans were cemented. It was agreed that Judd and Nima could borrow the car, drop Judd's gear off at his mother's house just ten minutes away, then "hang out" at David's house until it was time to hit a few of the local spots.

Nima said that before he went anywhere, he had to change his clothes. Nima invited Judd into his room to see his Chris Bonnington certificate, which proved he had climbed to twenty-four thousand feet on Everest, and to watch the end of some game show. I had been hoping that Judd wouldn't go into Nima's room, because it used to be Judd's room when he slept over—only then there had been no color TV, no wall-to-wall posters, no freshly covered sleeper-sofa, no desk, and no bookshelves.

About five minutes had gone by when I saw Judd tear out the front door. I thought that maybe seeing Nima's room was the last straw. But I was wrong. Judd went out to the car, fumbled through his duffel bag and came back in with a T-shirt for Nima. It was identical to the one Judd had on.

Seconds later they both came out. Nima was wearing his new Lafayette T-shirt. Judd was holding a package of Hostess Ding Dongs. Nima always had Hostess Ding Dongs on reserve to give to special people. I watched from the front window as they headed toward the car. Nima slung his arm around Judd's shoulder and gave it a couple of jerky squeezes just as Grover always did to Nima. Then the two hopped in the car and drove off.

The report the next day was interesting. For starters,

Nima had become one of the guys, although he stuck to Coca-Cola. Nima said that at one place called the Tin Whistle the bartender thought he was either Japanese or Korean. When Nima told the bartender that he was a Sherpa, the bartender said that he had never heard of a Sherpa before and wanted to know all about him. Nima was convinced that the bartender was just putting him on. I told Nima I doubted that, because before John and I went to the Himalayas, I was guilty of the same ignorance. Nima just chuckled, as if I were having him on as well.

Nima told me how he had met two girls in the bar, one with white hair (Nima always called blond hair white) and one with black curly hair. The one with white hair had gone to the same high school Nima was going to, but she went during the daytime. He had told her all about the time he put twenty-five cents into the school vending machine to get an apple and lost it. When he went to his teacher and said that he lost twenty-five cents, the teacher went back to the machine to try to get the quarter out. But he couldn't. His teacher said that one of the daytime students probably put "bad money" into the machine. Nima asked the girl with the white hair if she knew which student put bad money into the machine. The girl said that she had no idea. Nima asked her if she could find out and let him know.

I asked Nima if that was *all* they had talked about. He said no. He had also asked the girl about the six panes of broken glass at the south end of the school. The girl said that she didn't know who was responsible for that either.

The idea of vandalism was all very difficult for Nima to grasp. It is totally unheard-of among the Sherpas. I thought about what Sir Edmund Hillary had told us so many months earlier. "We counted over ten thousand hours of volunteer labor on the part of the Sherpas. They want to help themselves. That's what is so gratifying. . . . The schools are probably our most satisfying endeavor. Sherpas have a great curiosity.. They have a great respect for learning."

Beyond Nima's investigation into who vandalized *his* high school, we learned with a certain amount of horror that Judd and David had given into Nima's pleas and let him have a crack at driving the car. Judd had warned Nima not to breathe a word of this to anyone, especially John and me. But in all of Nima's excitement, he gave us a detailed account of his private driving lesson down at the Compo Beach parking lot. From what I gathered, Nima must have gunned the motor and raced it to 4,000 rpms and popped the clutch, as the car spun out like a LeMans racer. The only thing that saved them from a watery grave was Judd's quick application of the handbrake.

Fortunately, the preparations for Thanksgiving dinner got my mind off that potential disaster. Coming to dinner were our neighbors and close friends Sally and Don Blinn and their daughter, Nancy. It was Nancy who was soon to innocently play a very important part in Nima's life. Perhaps if Nancy had known just *how* important a part she was to play, she might never have walked through our front door.

# NINE

THE EVENING BEFORE Thanksgiving, I began preparing a traditional Thanksgiving dinner. While I was making a chestnut stuffing, Nima was setting the table, helping John carry logs in for the fireplaces, and generally tidying up the house—not that it needed any more tidying up. Nima saw to it that the place didn't have that lived-in look John found so comfortable. Sometimes I felt that living with Nima and John was like living with the Odd Couple. Although Nima never verbalized his intense dislike for clutter, his actions showed it. As soon as we would finish reading the newspaper, Nima would scoop it up, neatly fold it, and put it away. The same went for coffee mugs, dishes, ashtrays, jackets, shoes—anything that Nima felt would clutter things up. It drove John crazy. Several times he insisted that I talk to Nima about his compulsive neatness. But I never really saw the need for it. John said that he couldn't figure out how a rugged, salt-of-the-earth Sherpa from the foot of Mount Everest could turn into a Cleveland Heights housewife within months.

As I slid the last bit of stuffing into the turkey, I heard what sounded like a twelve-piece heavy metal rock band in our driveway. It was Judd and David to pick up Nima.

Almost immediately, a Fairfield Lumber baseball cap and Levi's jacket whizzed past the kitchen toward the front door. Before Nima had a chance to duck out, I headed him off in the hallway. I figured the reason Nima was in such a big hurry to join David and Judd was so I wouldn't have a chance to give them heck for Nima's Compo Beach driving lesson the night before. But I had promised Nima that I wouldn't say anything, if he promised he'd stay out of the driver's seat.

With one leg out the door, Nima said that they were going to Pizza n' Brew to pick up Traylor and then back to the Tin Whistle to "hang out" with Sean and Chris.

I was relieved the next morning to find Nima still in one piece. I couldn't get too much out of him concerning his second night on the town, other than that Westport Pizza used more cheese than Pizza n' Brew.

It was just about one o'clock when Nima, John, and I finally had everything ready for Thanksgiving Day dinner. While we were sitting in the living room waiting for the Blinns to show up, John was giving Nima and me a rather garbled textbook lecture on the origins of Thanksgiving. Then Nima told us about Mani-rimdu, also a late-November festival. He had described Mani-rimdu for us shortly after arriving at our home. Now, Nima added that Sherpas who give money to the lamas and bring food for the other pilgrims go up very high after they die, a lot higher than the Khambas, who just show up and freeload. The next year at Mani-rimdu, Nima was planning on giving the lama a hundred rupees, about ten dollars. He made sure we knew that the most Mingma had ever given at one time was thirty rupees, about three dollars.

Shortly after one o'clock, Don, Sally, and Nancy were at our front door. Just as I turned to introduce Nima to

Nancy, I discovered he was gone. Only seconds earlier, he had been leaning against the window, peering out, anxious for the Blinns to arrive. But now, as the Blinns were taking their coats off, there was no Nima to be seen. I looked toward his bedroom door. It was closed. Then I had a bleak thought. I knew that Nima had hung around at the window long enough to get a good look at Nancy. Maybe he just couldn't bring himself to a confrontation with the tall, attractive brunette.

And then an even more dismal thought entered my mind. Maybe Nima thought that John and I deviously arranged this meeting, so he stalked off to his room to sulk. But the more I thought about that the more unlikely it seemed. Nima wasn't the sulking type. In the past he had never shown signs of being even mildly irked at us, except when I didn't use the coupons he cut out. And we had given him plenty of opportunities to be more than irked—for instance John's constant nagging at him to invite the girl from Thailand over for dinner. Even then, Nima didn't seem annoyed at his suggestion; he simply explained that there were plenty of girls in the Solu Khumbu who liked him. He didn't need anyone over here complicating his life. (He didn't use quite those words.) John claimed that the only reason he kept suggesting that the Thai girl come for dinner was because every time the phone rang after six o'clock, she was always there on the line. I explained to John that just because she called Nima, it didn't mean Nima had any designs on her. Although Nima was always polite, he did nothing to encourage the conversation. He merely answered her homework questions, and that was that.

There was one thing that confused me now. Why did Nima wait until the Blinns were standing at the door before going to his room? And why, only minutes before they had arrived, did he tell me that he had taken out two large, color-illustrated books on the Himalayas to show Nancy? Now, with Nima gone, I glanced over toward the table where he had displayed the books. They were still there. But so were a lot of other things. On closer inspection, there were two pairs of scissors. One was a blunt-tipped child's pair. Next to the scissors was a stack of colored construction paper, a box of crayons, Elmer's glue, and a Dr. Seuss dictionary. It was a dictionary I had bought for Nima when he first arrived to help him associate the written word with the picture.

The playschool tools he had carefully arranged on the table had been the same things he had dragged out each time Geoffrey came over with his parents. Nima would sit for hours teaching him words, helping him cut and paste, showing him pictures of the Himalayas. But Nima had one house rule: no child was allowed to lay one sticky finger on the books. Nima would turn the pages himself.

It didn't take long to understand why Nima had suddenly disappeared. He had assumed that Sally and Don were bringing over a kid in a pinafore and Mary Janes. It apparently never occurred to him that their daughter would turn out to be a full-grown, attractive woman.

Twenty minutes after the Blinns arrived, I decided to send John after Nima. When John walked in, Nima was reclining on the sofa, his head propped up by a couple of pillows, a blanket shrouding him, watching the Thanksgiving Day Parade. Nima had the look of death in his eyes. In a faint voice, he told John that he had an upset stomach and that he thought it best if if he didn't move until his stomach settled. John, buying the act, came back out to get him an Alka Seltzer with extra pain relief.

After I explained to John and Nancy about the box of

crayons, John marched back to Nima's room and suggested that his stomach would settle just as quickly in the living room with the rest of us. Nima reluctantly followed John out.

Since that Thanksgiving Day, I have been trying to pinpoint the exact time Nima's upset stomach left and his butterflies arrived. The closest I could come was sometime after Judd arrived and before the coffee. By the time the pumpkin pie was served, Nima's eyes were glued to Nancy. He had by this time begun to tell us all about his close calls on Mount Everest, Kangchenjunga, and K–2. Ostensibly, the narration was for the benefit of all of us. But the only time Nima broke eye contact with Nancy, who was sitting to his left, was when one of us asked a question. We knew we were being used, but everyone seemed to enjoy hearing Nima dramatically reconstruct in vivid detail how he faced monsoon gales, treacherous ice falls, crashing boulders, and subzero temperatures. The only person who seemed to be getting a bit antsy was Don. I felt that although he was intrigued with the terrifying recreation, he was also anxious for Nima to wrap up the mountain talk so he could get in a few of his own airline anecdotes. Don was an airline captain, and never at a loss for semiamusing stories.

As soon as Judd had finished his dessert, he was more than ready to hit the Tin Whistle with Nima. But Nima had other things on his mind. He didn't even notice Judd leave. He was too busy telling Nancy how Grover and he were going to show the excavator where to dig the foundation for a new house. He asked Nancy if she had ever ridden on a bulldozer or a back hoe and told her he might be able to arrange something with Grover. I couldn't tell whether Nancy was interested in construction, but I could see that she was listening with patience and understanding.

By seven o'clock we were all pretty tired—except Nima. He had maneuvered Nancy away from the dining room table to a small table off the living room, where he had put the books on the Himalayas and toys. Once he made sure Nancy was comfortable, he gave her one of the books to read. Then he excused himself and leaped off to his bedroom.

A few minutes later, he swaggered out. Only now he had a whole different look about him. His hair had been slicked to one side and held in place with Gillette Dry Look, a man's hairspray he had seen advertised on TV. From the throat down he looked like Noel Coward. He had changed out of his T-shirt into a light blue tailored Arrow. Around his neck was the paisley ascot that I had picked up for him in London. Nima loved to wear a scarf; he felt that it completed the ensemble. When I had given him the silk ascot, he had said he was going to save it for the Air India flight home. He had obviously changed his mind.

Back at the table, he began pointing out to Nancy all the mountains he had climbed, and all the mountains Mingma hadn't climbed. Then Nima flipped open Chris Bonnington's book *Everest: The Hard Way* to the color photos. He pointed out a photo that included him, along with about a dozen or so other Sherpa guides. After Nima was certain that his face was fixed in Nancy's memory, he turned to page 196, ran his finger down to the middle of the page, and there, in black and white, was the name "Nima Dorje," village of Phakding, ice-fall porter.

After they pored through the Himalayan books, Nancy began telling Nima about her job as a graphic artist in North Carolina. Nima didn't hesitate to let Nancy know that he was no slouch himself when it came to art appreciation. He told her that I had taken him to the Whitney Art Museum in Stamford, Connecticut, just the week before.

As Nima was telling Nancy about a hunk of cement in

the shape of a head that he had seen at the museum, Nancy was shifting her eyes once too often to her watch. From where I was standing, Nancy looked as if she suddenly realized how late it was and that she had something important to do. But for Nima, he was doing what was important. Time did not exist.

Finally, Nima carried a few of the books back into his room, and Nancy took the opportunity to make a move for the coat closet. But in a flash Nima was back and tucked under his arm was a whole new supply of reading material. But Nancy had other ideas. She explained to him that although she thoroughly enjoyed meeting him and learning all about Sherpa guides, the Himalayas, Phakding, bulldozers, his family, his teahouse, and Mingma, it was late. She had to get back to her parents and make a phone call. (Sally and Don had been gone for over an hour.)

As Nancy slipped on her down vest, she apologized once again for not being able to stay and look through the new books. Then she told him why: she had promised her husband, who couldn't come up for Thanksgiving weekend, that she'd call him between eight and nine. And it was almost nine now.

This statement should have had a chilling effect on Nima. But it didn't. At first I thought he hadn't heard what Nancy had said. Maybe Nima thought that Nancy was talking about her brother or sister. But only a few seconds later Nima confirmed that he knew *exactly* what she had said. He went over to the bar, reached up, grabbed the telephone receiver, and called Nancy back from the front door.

"No problem," Nima said. "Nancy call husband from phone here."

On hearing that, my first inclination was to think that there was no romance, except for the one in my fertile imagination. I began to analyze Nima's moves. It was a fact that I had based this entire "romance" on Nima's actions toward Nancy. At no time did she ever romantically encourage Nima. She was attentive, but no more. It was also a fact that Nima had been a perfect gentleman.

Then I had second thoughts; even if Nima were enamored, he would remain a gentleman. Had this scenario been played out by Mingma it would have not taken on such a literary tone. Nima was different. And that's what puzzled me. He didn't have the typical attitude characterized by a lack of sexual inhibitions.

John and I had had several firsthand encounters with Mingma and Pasang and their amorous affairs. We also had Nima as moderator. He always kept us posted on what went on behind the tent flap. John and I didn't mind what Mingma and Pasang did on their time. But we did mind when—on this rare occasion—they excluded us from the comfort and safety of the inner campsite.

One such incident occurred at fourteen thousand feet, near Tengboche Monastery. As always, Mingma and Pasang and a couple of Sherpas they had picked up along the way had arrived at the campsite an hour ahead of us. By the time we got there, our tent had been strategically pitched about 100 yards from the campfire, the mess tent, and where they slept.

Mingma and Pasang had their reasons for placing our tent practically on the next mountain peak. We confronted Nima and he more than willingly confirmed what we had suspected.

"Mingma and Pasang," Nima said, "no want Memsahib and Sahib hear 'ho-ho-ho, ha-ha-ha-hee-hee-hee.' Mingma and Pasang all night times, laughs, hugs Sherpanis." Nima's obvious pleasure in relating gossip about the pajama party might have had something to do with Mingma and Pasang whooping it up while Nima was relegated to sleeping outside the tent, warmed only by his sleeping bag and a ratty sheet of plastic that kept the food pack dry.

John had warned Mingma more than once that our tent should be pitched as close to theirs as possible. He had his reasons—a reason that went back to the first night of our forty-day trek. Now when I think about it, the scene comes back as vividly as the day it happened.

Waking suddenly, I heard the outer flap of the small tent flutter. It was as if a brief and totally unexpected breeze had risen and died. It seemed strange in a way, because the night was exceptionally calm. But I was tired. We had climbed for a full eight hours that day, straight up the foothills on the first leg of our trek toward Everest. Our dome-shaped mountain tent was perched on a terrace, flat as a billiard table, chopped out by the hand of some Nepalese farmer probably centuries ago.

Next to me, zipped in his down mummy bag, John was sleeping off the agonies of the four-thousand-four-hundred-foot climb that day, all in the broiling Nepal sun. But now it was freezing. The tent fly was blanketed with a thick layer of snow. My total exhaustion made it hard to sleep. I unzipped the doorway of the tent and looked out. Some of the frost broke off and chilled the back of my neck.

The stars looked like diamonds on black velvet. I had never seen them look that way before. They gave off a shine that seemed to light the hills and the deep valley we had struggled up from. In the faint glow, some thirty feet away, I could make out the bare outline of our Sherpas' tent. The silence of the night was overwhelming, especially after the noisy streets of Kathmandu the previous week. But quite suddenly, the valley was pierced with the eerie shriek of a jackal on a distant ridge, an unearthly sound that brings shivers. It was immediately answered by a chorus of far-off dogs. When a jackal smells chickens in a farmyard and can't sink his teeth into them, he screams in frustration.

The sounds woke John. He stirred in his sleeping bag, yawned, but was not startled. "It's just a jackal."

"I'm scared," I said.

Mingma had warned us sharply not to leave anything outside the tent because of the jackals. "They will steal anything," he had said in his faltering English. "You must put everythings inside tent."

We had gone along with this willingly. It did not help our cramped situation, however. Our tent was jammed with four duffel bags, two large backpacks, camera cases, shoulder bags, canteens, tape recorders, and day packs that surrounded us like a fortress. There was literally no room to change positions once we zipped ourselves into our mummy bags.

The problem was that when we had to make our way to a nonexistent open-air john in the middle of the night, we ran into trouble. We had to fish out our boots, place them outside the tent doorway, wriggle our feet into them, and stumble off in an elaborate ritual for a relatively minor natural event, leaving the warmth of the sleeping bag and shivering in the cold.

John decided to perform this ritual at this time. But when he returned to the tent doorway, he stopped and pointed a flashlight down to the ground in front of the tent. "That's funny," he said. "My jogging shoes are outside here. I *know* I put them inside the tent when Mingma told us to."

I was getting sleepy again. I said, "Don't worry about it. You might have forgot in the confusion."

John agreed and he started to get back into the tent when

146

he suddenly turned and refocused his flashlight onto the ground. "Wait a minute," he said, "there's an empty duffel bag out here, too."

"Do you think Nima forgot to put it back into the tent?" I said.

"That's probably what happened." And he climbed back into the tent. Within minutes we were sound asleep.

We woke at six the next morning, when Pasang shoved two steaming mugs of tea through the tent flap. Putting the empty mug down, I reached down to find my clothes. John reached for his clothes too. But he couldn't seem to find his jeans, which he had carefully placed at the foot of his sleeping bag the night before.

Suddenly we both noticed a clean, two-foot-long slice an inch above the nylon floor of the tent. "Darnit," John said, "Mingma and Nima must have ripped the tent when they put it up last night."

But on closer inspection we noticed that it was no simple tear. It was a sharp, unmistakable knife cut. We studied it carefully. The tent had been surgically sliced, just six inches away from our feet as we slept. John's jeans, with his wallet in them, were gone. And it was not the jackals. Worse than that, our carefully assembled medical kit was gone, including most of the codeine, aspirin, Ace bandages, antibiotics, and a dozen other emergency remedies we had packed.

We called Nima over, showed him the sliced tent, and told him what had happened. His face clouded with distress.

"This should no happen in our land," Nima said. "I am sorry so much. You are both okay?" His voice was pained; his concern genuine. His eyes seem to reflect a bruise, as if it were inflicted on all his people. He called to Mingma, who came running over. He knelt down and examined the tent carefully.

"Someone with kukri knife," Mingma said. "Some bad peoples. No Sherpa."

"They cut right next to our feet," I said. "While we slept." It was not a comfortable thought.

"Is good thing you no wake up," Mingma said. Then he shook his head from side to side, in the distinctive way that only Sherpas do. "Just tent cut bad enough. Throat—no good."

I broke into tears. I had chills, and they were not from a fever. I wasn't sure, but I thought the same thoughts were going through John's mind as mine. Should we go on? Should we give up? What on earth were we doing here on the rim of this enormous valley, ravishingly beautiful as it was? Maybe our friends were right when they told us we were doomed before we started.

Mingma, Pasang, and Nima were more affected by what had happened than we were—if that was possible. They felt responsible. But they also felt helpless. They explained over and over that it was rare for something like that to happen. If we had been in Sherpa country, it would *never* have happened. The Sherpas have a strong sense of moral order. They believe that every action, from cutting down trees to stealing, is rewarded or punished in the next life.

At the time our tent was slashed, I had asked Nima if "Thou shalt not kill" meant anything to Buddhists. Having been robbed on the first night of our trek, I was worried about what the thieves would do for an encore. Nima made it clear that we had not been robbed by a Buddhist. However, he did say something about low altitudes and "no-good people," as if high altitudes and high morals went together.

Maybe Nima wasn't too far off. The higher you got in Sherpa territory, the less crime there was. I was glad of that. The thought of a knife cutting through our tent less than six inches from the soles of our feet was a chilling one. Ever since that time Nima and I had talked a lot about sin. I had once told him all the big sins of Catholicism, and he had done the same for me. Some Buddhist sins, he said, were to pluck flowers, talk behind someone's back (especially if you say untrue things), hit a child, argue, be cruel to animals, and cheat in trade.

Nima told us that committing those sins is of course not good, but it's not all that bad either. He explained why. If you cut down trees for a teahouse, that's a sin. But if you do something good the next day, then you will have canceled out the sin. For instance, if you help build a bridge, or tell a Khamba he's the same as a Sherpa, or take an egg to a Tamang, then you have gained merit, or what Nima called *sonan*. The sonan wipes out the sin, called *digba*.

I'm not sure what kind of digba Nima had in mind, if any, when he helped Nancy put on her parka back in Connecticut so many months after we had discussed sins, Khambas, and the great tent robbery. But I do know that on the way home, Nancy and Nima sat in the back seat of our car, and I felt like a chaperone at the high school senior prom. I thought about how Nima and I had always had good communication, especially when we talked about sins. Now I thought it was time to talk a little more about sins, especially the Commandment—thou shalt not commit adultery.

# TEN

The morning after Thanksgiving, John and I were still asleep when the phone rang. It was an elderly neighbor, who lives across the river, next door to the Blinns. She said that if I looked down toward the river I would see Nima on his bike riding around in circles. She wanted to know *why* he was on the lawn, in the rain, and on his bike. He was getting so close to the river that she was afraid he would accidentally skid in. I told her not to worry; Nima was used to rivers—rivers that would make ours look like a hot tub.

I did have to admit, though, that it looked awfully strange to see Nima sliding all over the wet lawn on his bike. I guess it looked strange to Don Blinn too. He was the next one to phone. He asked the same question. But that's not why Don had called. He wanted to take Nima to Kennedy Airport to board a 747, flight deck and all.

Before I put an end to Nima's circus act on the riverbank, I woke John and told him the news. Half asleep, he said, "Great." Then he yanked the covers up around his ears, turned over, and fell back into a deep sleep. I woke him again and told him that it was great, but it was also not so great. I reminded him of how Nima had been acting the night before with Nancy, and how Nima had given her a package of Hostess Ding Dongs. And how Nima only gives Ding Dongs to very special people, and how he was doing circles down at the river, obviously trying to get Nancy's attention. I told John that nobody in his right mind would ride a bike on slippery grass, unless of course that person has temporarily lost his sense—or, for lack of better words, is in love.

I told John that I was now *certain* that Nima was hooked on Nancy and that it wouldn't be right for us to encourage this infatuation. It would lead nowhere except to bitter disappointment. Male-female relationships among the Sherpas were completely different from what we know—or at least from what we openly practice. It was not at all uncommon for a Sherpa woman to have two husbands, just as men were allowed two or more wives in the Solu Khumbu. Nima told us of a friend who kept one wife in Kathmandu, where she ran his teahouse and took care of their two kids, and kept the other wife two weeks' distance away in the Solu Khumbu, where she tended the land. According to Nima, neither wife knew the other existed. I asked Nima why his friend kept the carefully guarded secret, especially since Sherpas were supposed to have open relationships. But Nima just chuckled and said that it was easier that way.

In spite of his friend's two wives, polyandrous marriage (a woman who has more than one husband) is much more common than polygamous marriage (a man who has more than one wife). A girl might marry two men at the time of *zendi,* or the wedding ceremony, if she is marrying into a household where there are two brothers; to keep the family property intact, the girl will simply marry both of them. If there happens to be a third brother, the middle one may join the local monastery. However, in recent years that is less common. Because of outside influences, Sherpa boys

*151*

are being lured away from the monastic life in favor of becoming guides or taking jobs in Kathmandu.

According to Sherpa custom, women are allowed no more than two husbands. Men, however, may have as many wives as they can afford. But the most frequent reason for a man taking on another wife is if the first marriage is childless, or if the marriage has produced no sons to carry on the family name.

To our Western eyes, these types of arrangements may seem doomed to end in jealous fiascos. But apparently this is rarely the case. After I learned about the women with two husbands, I wondered what it must be like at bedtime. According to the noted anthropologist Christoph von Furer-Haimendorf, it is all quite simple. The girl lies on the connubial mat in a secluded part of the house and the two brothers decide which one will luck out for the evening. Rarely does the girl make the choice. Nevertheless, some Sherpanis feel that there are definite advantages in polyandrous unions. Since young Sherpa men may be away a good part of the year, either trekking or trading, the girl is not often left alone for long stretches of time. Not only does this enhance her sex life, but her standard of living is twice as good as that of the woman who has only one husband.

If, however, a married Sherpa takes a lover, he or she is committing a sin against Buddhism. But, according to what Nima once told me, it is also a sin to chop down a tree, pick a wild flower, or make a child cry. There is a definite mechanical way of tripping up the sin system. The smart Sherpa has prepared for his or her fling by chalking up some *sonan,* or good deeds. The sonan will automatically wipe out the *digba,* or the sin, of having the affair.

The worst part of having an affair is getting caught, because if you are caught, then you are required to pay a *phijal,* or fine of fifteen rupees to the offended partner. After the phijal is paid and hands are shaken, all is forgotten. There are no grudges or jealous rages. An affair rarely leads to divorce and *never* leads to a jealous Sherpa committing a crime of passion. They simply don't exist in the Solu Khumbu. Of course, none of this explained why Nima's friend was so clandestine about his two wives and lives.

Nima did say that often a foolish Khamba is caught having an affair twice in a row. This doesn't mean you get any discount on the second phijal, but in almost all cases if someone is unfortunate enough to get caught immediately after paying the first phijal, the offended party will usually just say forget it. The person already had poor luck. Why compound his bad fortune with another fifteen rupees?

If affairs are easily solved, so are divorces. The Sherpas have the original no-fault divorce law. When a couple decides they no longer want to remain married, they invite the wife's close relatives to come to their home to take part in the official divorce ceremony.

After a few drinks of rakshi or chang, the husband will hold one end of a piece of thread; the wife's father or brother will hold the other. Then the thread is broken, symbolizing the end of the marriage. There are no lawyer fees, court costs, or mental aggravation—even in the case of one of the partners not wanting the divorce. The divorce is always granted. However, the partner who asks for the divorce is required to pay a fee of about five dollars as compensation.

As far as premarital sex is concerned, virginity for either partner is neither admired nor abhorred. In fact, it is taken for granted that if a young man and woman are going together they will also be sleeping together. The parents have no horror of premarital sex. This is not to say that promiscuity is the rule—at least not for the girl. The average Sherpa woman has at most two lovers before she marries.

One of the only drawbacks of a premarital affair is pregnancy. And it is more an inconvenience to the Sherpani, who may be needed in the field, than a social disgrace. In many cases, the couple will marry and legitimize the child, but there is no parental pressure to do so. If the boy and girl feel that they are not well suited, they will remain single. Just as there is no stigma attached to sexual relations, there is none attached to an unwed mother or an illegitimate child, called a *themba*. The themba child is entitled to inherit a portion of the father's estate, just as legitimate children are. Rarely will a father deny paternity. And even if he tries to, it won't do him any good. The mother's word is always taken.

Although all this had little to do directly with Nima and his passion for his new American friend, I could see enough of a link to try to wake John and get him on his feet. But he was barely reacting at all. I thought that maybe it was because he was still tired. But whatever the reason, he just didn't seem to be making the connection between what I had told him and Nima. He claimed that I was making a big deal out of an innocent crush. With that, I called Nima back from the river, where he was still riding his bike on the wet lawn. Once Nima was in the house, I said that Don was taking Nancy, Sally, and him to the airport.

It took Nima from 7:45 to nearly 8:30 to get himself put together. After showering, he styled his hair with my blow-dryer, which I now had to borrow back from him. Then he tried on about four different outfits before he got just the right one. He ended up country casual, dressed in khaki hiking slacks, a madras sport shirt, a gray sweater-shirt jacket, and his Adidases.

*Nima at the controls of a 747, with Nancy Blinn in the copilot's seat. He found JFK International Airport quite a contrast to the tiny landing strip chopped out of a mountainside at Lukla.*

At 8:30, when the Weston pharmacy opened, Nima and I drove down to get film for his Polaroid. Then Nima ran next door to Peter's, where he picked up two boxes of Morton salt. One was a gift for Sally and one was for me, because I wasn't able to go to the airport.

Don's gray jeep pulled up at nine o'clock sharp and returned to our driveway five hours later. By the time I heard the jeep and got downstairs, Nima was already bent over the dining room table, the camera case still slung over his shoulder, spreading out the Polaroid prints. He was as euphoric as an AP photographer who just caught Jackie Kennedy Onassis coming out of Woolworth's in a polyester print dress and hair rollers.

After the photos were in the right sequence, he ran up to John's office and brought him down. Nima went over each print as a photojournalist would with his editor. I was tempted to tell Nima that he didn't have to go into such detail: the pictures were self-explanatory. Finally, Nima asked me which picture I liked the best. I scanned the photos once again and then pointed to the one of him in the captain's seat, with his hand on the throttle, and Nancy in the copilot's seat with her face turned toward the camera. Nima said it was his favorite too.

I thought he was going to give me the picture, but I was wrong. He picked up a rather blurred print of Nancy and him standing in the cargo bin and told me to keep that. Then he picked up the good, clear print that we both thought was the best and he set it aside. That print, he said, would be going to Mingma through Big Boss Lhakpa.

At least Nima was predictable. He was still calculating moves to impress Lhakpa while he settled a few outstanding accounts with Mingma. As Nima scooped up the photos to take them into his room, he told us that Sally Blinn had asked if we could all have dinner at their house later. Nima said he hoped it was okay, because he had already accepted the invitation. He didn't stay long enough to hear if it was okay; apparently he had things to do and places to go. On the way to his room, he mumbled something about helping Don patch a leaky roof.

A few minutes later Nima came out dressed in his Grover Mills construction T-shirt and tool belt. Before I had a chance to ask him if he wanted some lunch, he was on the bike making a right onto River Road.

Before Nancy came into his life, Nima would not leave the house without a pit-stop in the kitchen. In fact, he would never pass the kitchen without at least a token trip to the refrigerator. Sometimes he would just open the door and stare into it, as if the bacon, eggs, and cheese were going to do a soft-shoe as they do in the commercials.

This time, however, Nima was in and out so fast I forgot to give him the letter that arrived while he was at the airport. I assumed it was from his Sherpa guide friend Ang Pemba, since it was on the same stationery the other letter he had written was on. I knew it wasn't from Lhakpa, who always answered Nima's letters on Mountain Travel stationery. And I was *sure* it wasn't from Mingma, who hadn't answered *one* of Nima's letters. I can't say that I blame him, all things considered.

Nima got home from helping Don patch the leaky roof with just enough time to shower and change for dinner with the Blinns. Before Nima got dressed, I gave him the letter, along with an envelope stuffed with coupons. Nima loved to get mail, and since not too much ever arrived for him, I made it a rule that all the mail addressed to boxholder and occupant went to Nima. He loved to muddle through the junk mail.

On the way to the Blinnses, Nima pulled his letter from the pocket of his new Levi jacket. "Nima get good letters from father," he said, waving the thin brown paper.

I was surprised to hear that the letter wasn't from Ang Pemba. I was more surprised that he said it was from his father. I had distinctly remembered Nima telling us back in the Himalayas that his father did not read or write. In fact, Nima said that was one of the reasons (along with discipline) he was sent to school—so there would be at least one person in the family who could read and write. Then I realized what Nima meant. His father had dictated the letter to someone who could write.

I turned around to the back seat as Nima clutched the letter two inches from his nose and translated.

"Father and mother say namaste to Memsahib and Sahib. Father say many, many thank for help good skinny son Nima get strong and no sick. Father say many good trades with Tibet. Father buy many new yak. Father have more yak than all Phakding. Father rich no like Mingma father. Father rich same like Ang Dali father."

During the entire translation, Nima did not once look up from the letter. There was something that just didn't ring true. As Nima paused to turn the page, I managed to slip in a question.

"Nima," I said, "that is a very good letter. Do you know who helped your father write it?"

"No, Memsahib. No Sherpa help father write letters. *Father* write letters."

Then he immediately pushed the thin paper back in front of his face and continued to translate. "Father say Mani-rimdu many goods. Father give one hundred rupee for lama. Mother give chicken and egg to poor cheap Khamba. Lama say to father, 'Father and mother go up very high at dying times.' Lama ask how is good, sick, skinny son Nima? Father say to lama that son Nima is no sick. Nima is strongs, many good carpenter, many good student, many good clothes." Then Nima wrapped up the letter by saying that the lama had told his father that Memsahib, Sahib, and Dr. Altbaum were good same like Sherpas.

On the way into the Blinnses' barn-red clapboard house, Nima asked if I thought Don and Sally would like to hear what his father had written. John pinched my arm and cast a sidelong glance that could have damaged his peripheral vision. I told Nima that I was sure that they'd enjoy it.

We didn't even have a thing in our hands before Nima was waving the letter about, anxious to get on with it. It was all so obvious. Nima was letting Don and Sally know that he came from a first-rate family. He translated the letter just as he had for us, but this time he added one extra touch. He said something about his father being very busy as *phar-kimi*. Of course none of us knew what "pharkimi" was.

Nima looked a little surprised that all of us could be so ignorant of Sherpa politics, but he generously explained the role of a pharkimi in the Solu Khumbu culture.

According to Nima, if two Khambas get drunk on chang and then get into a fight, and the fight is not resolved, a pharkimi is summoned to act as a go-between. The pharkimi prevents the whole village from suffering because two squabbling Khambas can't make up. (When I asked Nima if two Sherpas ever have to summon the aid of a pharkimi, he gave me an incredulous look, hesitated a moment, then reluctantly said yes, but usually they're Khambas.)

Nima went on to tell us that the pharkimi settles the dispute by inviting the two screaming Khambas to his house, where he hears both sides. It is then up to the pharkimi, who has been elected a village official because he is very respected and wise, to decide who should apologize to whom. Once that is established and the apology made, they all drink a glass of chang. The chang symbolizes the washing away of the dispute. According to Nima, the only problem is that sometimes it is difficult for the pharkimi to keep the Khambas at one glass of chang. And since the pharkimi is the one who is footing the bill, it can run into some bucks. Nima stressed that the pharkimi gets no rupees, eggs, or potatoes for his services. He does it just because he is a good, smart man.

Finally, Nima put down the letter so that he could help himself to some cheese. As he did so, I glanced down at the letter. There in the left-hand corner of the stationery was the date—written in English. That was my final clue. The letter could not have been written by his father. Nima's friend Ang Pemba always wrote the date in English.

I couldn't tell what the Blinns thought of Nima's letter, but I read in John's face what I was feeling in my own heart: a sandbag. If John and I hadn't been so oblivious to Nima's nonphysical needs, he would not have had to invent that letter. We had been so involved with Nima's health that we had overlooked Nima's need to feel important and to be recognized as a worthwhile human being from a first-rate family.

While Nima showed Nancy his "father's" letter, I told the Blinns about our visit with Nima's family in Phakding: about what a fantastic cook Nima's mother was, and how Nima had the best house in Phakding, and how his father had been out on a trading caravan to Tibet, so we hadn't had a chance to meet him. But anyone who gave one hundred rupees at Mani-rimdu time must be indeed a very important person. Nima was pretending not to be listening, but when I said that his father had eight yak, Nima immediately corrected that to twelve.

I knew one thing: I would never tell anyone that the letter had not been from his father. If Nima wanted us to believe that his father could write, then that's how we would leave it.

Dinner at the Blinns' that night turned out to be a rerun of the Thanksgiving dinner. The only difference was that the following day Nima would not be seeing Nancy. She was returning to North Carolina. Several times during the evening, I overheard Nima making a few desperate last-ditch attempts to encourage Nancy to postpone her trip. Once was when Nancy was in the kitchen making coffee. Nima followed her in and said something to the effect that it was a shame she wouldn't have a chance to meet Grover and the guys. He was almost certain that if she stayed he could get Grover to arrange a ride on Big John's backhoe. They could even go see Louie at the deli for a bagel and egg. Nancy answered Nima by reminding him that she had been away from her husband for nearly a week. It was time that she go back.

Nima nodded and started to walk back toward the dining room table, but then he stopped. He asked Nancy if she knew how much her husband made per hour. Nancy seemed surprised by the financial question, but not annoyed. She told him that she had really never stopped to work out his hourly wages. He then asked Nancy if her husband had ever buggy-lugged four tons of twelve-inch cement blocks across a footbridge onto an island. Nancy said no. A totally self-satisfied look came over Nima's face as he went on to tell Nancy that he had done just that only days earlier.

As we left, Nancy casually asked us all to drop by and see her if we ever found ourselves in North Carolina. I had no idea how literally Nima would take that particular social nicety. I should have, considering how literally he had taken other such clichés.

When Nima had first arrived, for example, and someone would ask him how he was, he had the habit of telling the person *exactly* how he was—down to the precise dosage of the medicine he was taking. After I noticed Nima doing that a few times, I explained to him that "How are you?" was just a greeting. People don't actually expect you to tell them how you are. What they did expect you to say was "fine," or "not bad," or even "hanging in there." I told Nima that another local cliché was "Let's have lunch." It didn't mean that they really wanted to have lunch; it was just a way to say good-bye. The best way to deal with that was merely say, "Yes, we'll have lunch." Then you keep on walking.

Several weeks later, with Nancy long gone, Nima and Grover enthusiastic about a new job on Saugatuck Shores, Judd back at college, and John beginning research on a new book, I found myself in the kitchen making brownies.

Nima loved my brownies. Usually, before I even managed to get the frosting on, he had helped himself to half the tray. But not this time. The brownies were in honor of his class Christmas party. Mr. Mastroberadino had made Nima official party planner, which meant that Nima would plan the menu, delegate who brought what, and figure out how much each student should spend. Nima said he probably got the job because he was the only one who could pull it off. (Part of Nima's job as Sherpa guide entailed helping the sirdar buy the food for expeditions.) In addition to planning the menu, Nima would also organize the entertainment. My part in the preparations had been to drive Nima from Peter's to the A&P to Shopwell to the Grand Union, so he could check out where each student could get the best deal. I was tempted to tell Nima that it was a waste of time, that all the stores here had basically the same prices. Beside that, the gas we were using was eating into the delicate balance that was my profit and loss. But I didn't say anything. Instead, I thought about how Nima had taken us all over the map in the Himalayas to visit the high-altitude monasteries.

With Nima as our guide, we had visited many. At no time did he say that one monastery was the same as the next one. Even when we yelled at him for being a lousy translator, he never complained. And we needed that translation because of the book John was planning to write. The fact is, we never got enough research for him to write it.

Now, whenever I think about that unwritten book I think about Tengboche Monastery. The low, sprawling gomba sat at thirteen thousand feet like a framed jewel. Surrounding the holy grounds were Mount Everest, Nupste, Lhotse, and Ama Dablam—the highest mountain range in the world.

Before arriving at Tengboche, we had been to five other monasteries, but none seemed to radiate this aura of mysticism. Perhaps Ernst Haas, the famous photographer, was right when he said that the highest mountains seem to have inspired the highest level of human spirit. I am not referring to my own spirit. The nausea, the headaches, and the raging cold dragged me down to the lowest level of human spirit. But John and I were not counting on ourselves for any deep insight into the spiritual world. We were counting on the high lama who resided at Tengboche. We were told that he could impart great wisdom to us.

As we trudged upward toward thirteen thousand feet, the great Tengboche Monastery suddenly came into view. Beside it were many tall poles with prayer flags whipping in the wind. There were dozens of small white buildings clustered about the main temple. Together, they sat majestically overlooking the valley, carved and pounded out by the rushing waters of the Beni Khola over the centuries. As we drew nearer, the tinkle of bells was heard above the wind. It was a magical sound.

Just outside the gateway that led up to the main temple and the quarters of the High Lama, Nima stopped us. We sat down on some rocks as he instructed us on the protocol to follow. He handed us each a prayer scarf—a white piece of gauze some three feet long and ten inches wide. He said that if we wanted to make a contribution, we were to fold the donation into the scarf. Then we were to hand it ceremoniously to the lama when he greeted us, holding it over the left arm, and bowing as we did.

As Nima led the way, we continued up a steep rocky path through the outside gate, then stopped at a small house while Nima talked with a monk who seemed to be the gatekeeper. We could continue, Nima told us, after they had tied up the ferocious Tibetan mastiffs in the courtyard beyond.

Soon the monk returned to lead us through a narrow tunnel into the courtyard. Finally, we reached what appeared to be the back door of the monastery. A lama in a claret-colored robe and a kindly face creased with age opened it. He stood to one side to usher us in and smiled broadly, revealing a set of brilliant white teeth. Then he closed the door. We were suddenly enclosed in pitch blackness.

We were instructed to remove our boots. In a moment, I could see a dark, narrow wooden stairway. It gave me the feeling I was in an amusement park funhouse. After we creaked up the stairway, we plunged into another large, dark room that looked like a kitchen in a medieval castle, with its low ceilings and enormous beams. There was a row of carved wooden tables along one wall, which contained the only window.

The lama bowed and swept his long, sleeveless arm toward the bench behind the tables. Then he glided toward a charcoal brazier that was burning at the end of the room and squatted on a low seat beside it. Along the wall opposite us hung a row of huge copper pots and caldrons. Next to that was a large, blackened fireplace where two large copper tea kettles were steaming. Attending them was an elderly Buddhist nun, who smiled toothlessly at us, bowing deeply and gracefully.

To our left were two other nuns. They were enthusiastically polishing bronze teacups and copperware with grimy rags, and laughing with each other as they did so.

No sooner had we sat down than one of the nuns scuffled toward us with teacups. They were filled with steaming buttered tea. This traditional beverage is served everywhere in the Himalayas, and it is a discourtesy to refuse it. It tasted like salty butterscotch, and although I hate butterscotch, I sipped it anyway.

I don't know how long we waited on the hard benches drinking tea before the Holy Man entered. Because of the cold, dank atmosphere it seemed like hours, but it was probably only fifteen minutes before he could be seen descending a dark, narrow staircase at the far corner of the room. He was wearing a claret-colored robe just as the other lama, but his had sleeves. He was much younger looking than I had expected, probably in his early fifties. As the lama neared, Nima nudged us to stand and bow namaste. Then I presented him with the prayer scarf just as Nima had instructed.

After the ritual, I took out my tape recorder, a pad and a pencil, and the interview began.

"Nima," John said, "would you ask the lama why they build their monasteries so high up? Is it because they feel closer to God up here?"

John and I had learned from other monasteries we had visited that it was useless to ask long, involved questions. Something always got lost in the translation. Nima did his best. But he only had a basic understanding of English. And we had no understanding of the Sherpa language. The interviews up until this point had, at best been frustrating. We had received no solid answers to anything we had asked.

Nima turned to the lama and repeated John's question. The lama then said something to Nima, and they both looked at us with puzzled expressions.

"Sahib," Nima said, "lama want to know why you come to this country."

Since John had a tendency to get too wordy, I spoke. "Nima, tell the lama that my husband and I come here to learn about Truth." At that point I checked my tape deck to make sure that it had picked up our voices. Then I went back and tried to explain as simply as I could that we were comparing Eastern and Western thought for a book John intended to write.

Nima and the lama began talking back and forth, as if a tape recorder were on fast-forward. Then Nima said, "Memsahib, lama ask to see you tape machine."

I handed it over to Nima. Nima was as familiar with how it worked as we were. His favorite pastime had been to sing Sherpa folk songs into it, and then revel in the sound of his own voice. Nima began smugly demonstrating the machine to the lama. He had the lama speak into it, and then he replayed it. When the lama heard his own voice played back, there was a great outburst of laughter.

I felt slightly irreverent laughing in such holy territory, especially since we were so close to the temples that we could hear the faint hum of the monks chanting. But Nima told us later that there was nothing wrong with laughing.

Finally Nima returned the tape deck to me. It appeared that the lama was so excited at hearing his voice played back that he forgot our question. So I repeated it to Nima. He repeated it to the lama. Then the lama gave Nima his answer.

"Yes," Nima translated. "They are five hundred meters closer to God."

John's eyes darted in my direction. We didn't need to speak.

Out of pure stubbornness I asked another question. "Nima, ask the lama, 'What is Truth?'" I explained that we were fed up with man's inhumanity to man. Also, I added, my husband and I were not thrilled with the threat of a nuclear war, and with the Soviet and the U.S. governments pouring more and more money into nuclear arms, when the world was already twenty-eight minutes away from total annihilation. I looked at my watch and tapped it to emphasize the twenty-eight-minute point.

Nima translated, and the lama spoke through Nima. "Memsahib, lama like to see you watch."

I took off my diver's watch. Nima began demonstrating the various dials. He had learned about watches from other expeditions. In fact he wore a beat-up Omega that had no crystal and only one hand. The lama studied the watch with immoderate glee before returning it.

"Nima," I said, "did you ask the lama if he could tell us what Truth is?"

After several seconds Nima spoke. "Lama say, 'Truth is Truth.'"

At that, John, Nima and I thanked the holy lama for his time and left the sacred grounds. Exhaustion had replaced any journalistic curiosity we had left. The following day we headed back toward the Lukla airstrip to end our forty-day trek.

The afternoon before Nima's class Christmas party, Grover had dropped him off an hour early so that he could have enough time to get properly natted out. That morning I helped Nima lay out what he was going to wear. He was torn between a new pair of Levi's or corduroy Alpine knickers. He finally went with the Levi's, because he had a green shirt and red crewneck sweater with a green bandana that he thought would be appropriately Chrismassy. The only problem was that he was going to have to turn up the jeans because they were too long. He was a little concerned that they wouldn't hang well. When John heard that, he became enraged. He told Nima that he had turned from a rugged

Sherpa into a finicky preppy. When Nima left the room, John said that he was seriously concerned about Nima's personal fastidiousness and his ability to adapt once back in the mountains. John felt we were doing Nima a grave disservice by indulging his whims. Since John felt so adamant about this, I made certain that he was not around when I shortened Nima's Levi's.

As I was frosting the brownies, Nima came into the kitchen and reminded me that he had to meet Mr. Mastroberadino at school an hour before class. They had to set up a record player and get the tables laid out for the food. I told Nima that the brownies would be ready in time, but they weren't going to be half as good as the ones I usually made. This was his fault. Nima had refused to spring for the walnuts and chocolate chips. Each student had a three-dollar limit and he had already gone over his by twenty-two cents because the coupon that he thought was for frosting turned out to be for Duncan Hines angel food cake mix.

While I was cleaning up the mess, Nima was cutting the brownies into small squares, making sure that each student would have exactly two each. As he was doing the precision cutting, he told me about some of the more colorful characters in his class. His favorites were the Italian man with the "bald head and the bright ties," the Jewish lady with the "double-colored" hair, and the black lady with the "curly hair and glasses." They were most like Sherpas because, he said, they were always joking around—and they were also the smartest.

Nima said that during the coffee breaks it was always the Italian, the black, the Jew, and the Sherpa who hung out. Nima didn't even mention the girl from Thailand. When I asked about her, he said that she was good like Sherpani, but not good like Nancy.

That was the first mention of Nancy in over a week. I thought Nima had laid her memory to rest, but he obviously hadn't.

"Memsahib," Nima said, "think good idea Nima take bus North Carolina say, 'How's it going?' to Nancy?"

"Nima," I said, "you *know* Nancy has a husband."

"No problem, Memsahib. Nima say, 'How's it going?' to Nancy husband too."

I thought I had convinced Nima that in this country we don't pursue another's spouse, at least not openly. Twice I had gone through the whole cultural spiel. The first time was the day Nancy left. Nima wanted to drop her a line inviting her back up for Christmas. The second time was a week later. He wanted to send her his picture, plus a Xerox copy of the page in Chris Bonnington's book with his name on it. Monogamy was a concept that just didn't sink in.

Now, for the third time, I stressed that *morally* it was not right, *logistically* it was too far, and *financially* it would wipe him out. Nima understood two out of the three.

We dropped Nima off for the Christmas party at exactly 7:30. John got out of the car to give Nima a hand with the two plates of brownies and three Beatles albums, but Nima insisted that he could manage alone. Before Nima got out he reminded us for the fifth time that the party should be wrapped up by ten, but we shouldn't come back until ten-thirty. That would give him a half hour to help Mr. Mastroberadino clean up and collect a delinquent eighty-six cents from one of the students. After we were certain that Nima had made it inside the school, we drove on for dinner.

Over dinner I filled John in on the continuing saga of Nima and Nancy. John still acted as if Nima merely had an innocent crush on Nancy—a crush that would go nowhere. I told John that this innocent teenage crush was bound and determined to hop on the first Greyhound headed south, unless of course we spelled it out that the farthest south he was going to get was New York City.

It was at that point that we were hit with a scheme. When we picked Nima up from his Christmas party, John would lay the bad news on him: He could not go down to North Carolina. Then before Nima had a chance to protest, I would come in with the good news: we were taking him into New York City, somewhere he had been dying to go. We would buy Nima off with New York City.

Nima had estimated that the party would be over by ten, and the cleanup by ten-thirty. John and I pulled into the parking lot a little before ten-thirty, and exactly five minutes later Nima appeared at the school door. When he saw our car, he grinned, showing practically every one of his three-layered toothpaste teeth. That was a good omen.

The party had been a success. Nima said that it had started slowly, but he livened it up by lecturing on the hazard of running one thousand five hundred feet of fixed rope across the Upper Snow Field toward the South Summit Gully on Everest, and then by teaching Sherpa dances. Even the old lady from Lithuania with thick legs danced. I asked Nima if they sang Christmas songs. He said Mr. Mastroberadino wrote "Jingle Bells" on the blackboard and the class sang it ten times while Annatchka played the flute.

As it turned out, the anticipation of a trip to New York City was no replacement for Nancy. Penny was the replacement. The evening before we were to take Nima to New York, we went to a Christmas party given by Ann and David Tolson. Nima was a hit, as he was wherever he went. On the ride back home, Nima summed up the party. "Good foods, good talks, good daughter." The daughter Nima was referring to belonged to the Tolsons. There were many similarities between Nancy and Penny. The most important was that they were both "tens"—another concept Nima had borrowed from Grover.

Nima had spent the evening at the Tolsons in much the same way he had spent Thanksgiving with the Blinns. The first half of the evening, Nima held the guests spellbound as he relieved his death-defying escapades on Mount Everest, Annapurna, and Kangchenjunga. The second half of the evening, he somehow managed to maneuver Penny to a secluded corner between the Christmas tree and a potted fern, where he told her what he had been up to for the last eighteen years.

Before Nima went to bed that night, he said that perhaps John and I had been right about Nancy. She did live too far away. And she did have a husband. On the other hand, he told us that Penny lived only a short bike ride away, she was only nineteen, and she wasn't married. I didn't have the heart to tell Nima that right after the holidays she was returning to Tufts University near Boston.

The rush of the holiday season was good in one respect: it didn't give us too much time to contemplate the end of Nima's visit, which would come in less than three months. As it was, John and I had talked for many painful hours about extending his visa. But in spite of all of our talk, we always ended up with the same conclusion: the longer we postponed his departure, the more difficult his readjustment to the Himalayas would be.

To ease the pain of his leaving, we had to keep reminding ourselves that our original intention had been to bring Nima here to get well, learn better English, and take a course in first aid, knowledge of which was badly needed in the remote mountain villages of the Solu Khumbu.

All of those expectations were being fulfilled. As long as

Nima continued to take his medicine, he would remain in perfect health. He now weighed in at 124 pounds, nearly a forty-pound weight gain. His English had improved almost as much as his health and so had his slang. Nima's vocabulary was a strange mixture of Grover's, John's, and mine. From Grover, he picked up a New England twang, along with practical everyday language. From me, he picked up a vocabulary that was strictly for comfort and ease. And from John, he had picked up something akin to the Queen's English, had she been born and raised in Philadelphia.

Nima told us Mr. Mastroberadino had whispered to him during a coffee break that he was one of the best speakers in the class. Since that time, Nima had begun to spend more time on his homework so he wouldn't let his teacher down. And because both John and I praised Nima whenever he dropped a new word, he dropped a lot of new words.

As far as the first aid lessons went, we decided that it would be best if we waited until Nima finished his English course. That way he wouldn't have to divide his concentration between the two subjects. It would also be fresher in his mind when he went back to the Himalayas a month later.

Whenever John and I started to feel low about Nima leaving, we realized that his visit had been more productive and positive than we ever could have hoped. Aside from his health and English, he had surprised us by becoming quite a skillful apprentice carpenter. And he surprised himself by earning eleven hundred dollars, a giant wad of "big ones" that he had stashed somewhere in the house. Nima changed his hiding place as often as he changed his clothes. I warned him that one of these days he was going to lose it, but he said Sherpas always do this with their money. Only a Khamba would forget where he hid it. With the money, the carpentry skill, and—most important—his enthusiasm, Nima had all the ingredients necessary to make his dream teahouse come true.

Nima showed no sign that the thought of his eventual departure would dampen *his* Christmas spirit. He had too much to do. And his room showed it. I suggested that he go easy on the presents, but he said he was worried that someone might give him a gift and he wouldn't have one to give in return. Nima didn't volunteer to tell me what was inside all the neatly wrapped packages. But from their familiar size and shape, half of them looked suspiciously like boxes of Morton salt.

Nima's excitement was further heightened by the fact that Judd would be home from college in two days. Just before we had left for the Tolsons' party, Judd had phoned and asked to speak to Nima. After much hilarity on Nima's end, and a final assurance that he would keep his evenings open for pizza and brew and the Tin Whistle, Nima said, "Take it easy, ya hear," and hung up.

Now, hours after Judd had phoned and twenty minutes after we had come home from the Tolsons' Christmas party, I gave Nima the alarm clock he had asked for. He wanted to make sure he got up in plenty of time for our trip to New York. I told Nima to be prepared to leave the house no later than eight, so we could catch the eight-twenty train. Nima didn't know what he was more excited about: seeing New York City or going on his first train ride.

The excitement was with us too, but there was still the shadow of Nima's eventual leaving that hung over the tinsel and holly Nima and I had laboriously splashed about the house. What we didn't anticipate, though, was the sudden, disastrous shock that hit just before we were to leave for New York.

# ELEVEN

THE FOLLOWING MORNING when I called Nima for break-fast, he came out of his room still in his white terrycloth bathrobe. His face was the same shade as his robe.

"Nima," I said, "why aren't you dressed? Are you sick?" He looked a notch beyond sick.

Nima said that, because of the excitement of going into New York, he didn't even need the alarm clock. He woke up at five-thirty and was unable to fall back asleep. He got up, went into the kitchen, and fixed himself a bowl of Fruit Loops. After the cereal, he wrote a letter to his mother. In the letter, he was telling her how much money he had saved. He couldn't remember if he had 1,126 "big ones" or 1,129, so he went to the linen closet, pulled away the towels, and removed his little safe. When he unlocked it, he found it was empty.

Nima didn't panic. Often he would try to trip a potential burglar up by putting his money in a Maxwell House Coffee can, or in a pillowcase, or even inside a sock stuffed into the toes of his work boots. He immediately began searching his other hiding spots—with no luck. In desperation, he went to hiding spots that he had staked out but never actually used. There was no money to be found anywhere.

As I listened to Nima, I began fuming. We had bought Nima that small safe for this very reason, so he wouldn't keep switching hiding places and forget where he had hidden his money. I asked Nima if he thought the money could be in any other room. He said no.

Suddenly, I smelled the muffins burning. I looked at my watch. It was after seven. I told Nima to get dressed and have some breakfast; we would search his room from top to bottom after we got back from New York. Then it took everything I had to console him. I told him not to worry. The money had to be in his room. It just didn't walk away. I told him we certainly didn't have any burglars in the house. They would have taken a lot more than his money; our electric typewriters, for instance. I also reminded him that our dog was a killer poodle when it came to unwelcomed intruders.

When John came downstairs a few minutes later and I told him that Nima had misplaced his money, he let Nima have it as he had never done before. Essentially John said that same thing I was thinking: it was stupid to take money out of the safe and Nima was pigheaded for not letting us put it into American Express travelers checks. He deserved to misplace it. Then John softened. He suggested the same thing I had—that Nima get dressed, have breakfast, and stop worrying. We would find the money after we came back from New York. Nima nodded, started for his bedroom, but before he got there he turned back to us.

"Nima," I said, "don't worry. We'll find the money tonight."

"Memsahib, Sahib, no find money. Money no in Nima's room."

Then he told us the *whole* story. The Saturday before, he had taken the wad of 1,126, maybe 1,129, dollars into

Westport. He wanted to finish his Christmas shopping. The last time he clearly remembered seeing the money was when he paid for gifts at the Westport Sport Mart. He said that when the salesgirl handed him his change he put the coins in his pocket and the bills went with the wad. But the wad was too bulky to fit into his wallet. He thought he had put it into one of the five bags he had with him.

He had to run to catch the last minibus back to Weston. When he got to the minibus station, he had a five-minute wait, so he sat down on the bench and began rearranging the gifts into different bags to make them easier to carry. Nima said that's when he was afraid the money had slipped out of one of the bags.

Any annoyance I felt toward Nima for not using his safe suddenly dissolved. I felt nothing but sorrow for him. The money he had worked so hard for was gone. He had saved enough to build his teahouse and then some.

Nima's eyes began to well up with tears. I tried to think of something to say, but everything I thought of seemed so vacuous. John was equally silent. Finally he put his arm around Nima's shoulder and led him to the kitchen table. John told Nima that although it was a costly mistake, it could have been a lot worse. At least he had his health. That was the important thing. Nima tried to be brave, but his face seemed pained, and that hurt us almost as much as he was hurting.

As we ate breakfast, John, Nima, and I talked about postponing the trip to New York. But in the end we decided not to. Nima still really wanted to go. John thought it might help get our minds off the money and I agreed.

At a quarter to eight, Nima and I were down at the river giving Boodles her last run as we waited for John to get ready. We must have been sitting mutely at the picnic table a good ten minutes when Nima began telling me about the time Mingma had been in a crowded Kathmandu market and a thief had slashed his back pocket and robbed him of three thousand rupees. Suddenly I looked up. It was John. He was jogging toward us. As he got nearer I noticed something lumpy in one hand. The lump looked suspiciously like a sock. And the sock looked suspiciously like Nima's. It was the wad. John had found the 1,126, maybe 1,129 dollars.

Nima was saying a lot—all of it in the Sherpa language. But his body language was universal. In one jerky move, he grabbed the sock, did a Sherpa high jump, and bear-hugged us. John had found the sock wedged behind Nima's dresser drawer. It was pushed so far back it came out almost unrecognizable.

On the way to the train, Nima made up for a lot of lost words. He said that he had acted like a real Khamba, misplacing his money like that. John corrected him. He told him that he had acted like a bullheaded Sherpa. No Khamba would be so stubborn after losing his money to *still* argue against putting it into travelers checks. Nima just couldn't relate to travelers checks. I don't know how many times we tried explaining to Nima that they were the same as money, but even better. If he lost the checks, they would be replaced. Nima didn't get the logic. As we pulled into the station parking lot, John told Nima that there was nothing left to discuss. On Monday morning we were going to the Union Trust and convert the wad into travelers checks.

We stood on the platform waiting for the train, along with about a third of Westport. John and I didn't see anyone we knew. But Nima did. One was an elderly lady, a client of Grover Mills whose house was being remodeled on Saugatuck Shores. The other was a waiter from a local restaurant. Nima always had something to say to everyone he knew, characteristic of all Sherpas. Nima reminded the elderly lady *not* to remove the plastic from the bags of insulation. If they got wet, he warned her, they'd be good for nothing but a trip to the dump. Then he explained to the waiter that the reason why Grover and he hadn't been in for lunch was because they were still at the Darien job.

It was only 8:30 A.M. and I was already exhausted. The shock of the lost money, then the excitement of finding the money, combined with the anticipation of a full day in New York during the Christmas rush made me wish we had postponed the trip. One of the things I dreaded the most was the shopping excursion to Kreeger's, a complete mountain-climbing store, where Nima was going to pick out a parka—maybe.

Since the beginning of November, Nima and I had been in search of the "perfect parka." We hit practically every store in Connecticut. But we always returned empty-handed. Nima had a pattern to his shopping. First he would try on all jackets in his size. This included boys' sizes and mens' sizes. Then he would start the elimination process— by color, texture, durability, pockets, zippers, length, and general all-around style. After the first dozen or so jackets had been eliminated, the salespersons, regardless of how patient, would invariably walk away. But when Nima had narrowed his selection down to roughly half a dozen, he would locate the cringing clerks and bombard them with so many questions about each jacket that even the manufacturer would have been hard put to answer some of them. And just when I thought Nima had actually made a choice he would say, "Thank you. We'll be back."

Now, as the train doors slammed closed, the three of us made our way to facing seats at the front of the car. Nima's eyes grew luminous; his smile broadened. It was hard to believe this was his first train ride. As I watched Nima snap his head from right to left, taking in the countryside, rows of houses, and the outskirts of the city, I thought back to nearly a year earlier when John and I got our first glimpse of Nima's country.

We flew over the Ganges plains of India, with its twisting rivers and fertile fields. Gradually hummocks began to appear, and then hills. In less than an hour, the hills steepened into mountains, jagged and gray, but with no snow cover. It was too misty to see ahead to the giant Himalayas, but the foothills looked formidable enough. Soon the terraced sides of the wide bowl of Kathmandu Valley slipped down from the southern mountains, forming with the northern foothills the green, level floor of the bowl. The terraces chopped out of the mountainsides showed up like the lines of a contour map.

Kathmandu, a city of half a million, sprawled in the distance, an ill-defined landscape in the hazy February sun. It was hard to realize that the verdant and lush valley below us had remained a forbidden kingdom up until thirty or so years ago. Its long isolation had only been broken in the early 1950s, when exotic and mysterious Nepal was suddenly confronted with the jet age.

When we emerged from Grand Central, Nima stared up at the skyscrapers the way we had stared at the awesome cluster of snow-covered peaks surrounding Everest. He walked up Park Avenue and across West Forty-sixth Street, toward Kreeger's, in a daze. More than once he stepped into the street toward a kamikaze taxi driver; more than once we had to yank him back. He seemed to want to look nowhere but up, toward the tops of the buildings.

At Kreeger's, the shopping marathon began. But when Nima went into a pantomime in front of the mirror that seemed to indicate that he liked one parka more than the four he had already tried on, John grabbed the forest-green jacket, gave it to the salesman, and told him to bag it. Nima was particularly bothered by John's willingness to pay the sticker price. But he wasn't too vocal, probably because I had warned him that John wouldn't tolerate indecision or bargaining.

After taking in the Radio City Music Hall, Christmas decorations at Lord & Taylor, and F.A.O. Schwarz, we approached the Pan Am Building, perched high above Grand Central. When we told Nima that we were going to have lunch on the top floor, his eyes scaled the sheer sides of the building and he said, "Memsahib, Sahib, okay to climb, many, many step?" The only time Nima had ever been in an elevator was at the Norwalk Hospital. But he had been so sick, I doubted he even remembered.

We took the express elevator to the Skyclub Restaurant on the fifty-seventh floor. Seconds later, when we got off what Nima called the "fast box" and he looked down, he could barely get it through his head that the toylike cars and taxis below were real. He said that the view looked exactly like the miniatures from the F.A.O. Schwarz Christmas display window. Luckily, the excitment did not affect his appetite. He ordered the Skyclub special and two Cokes to wash it down. In between, he took several trips to a nearby window to give himself some reality testing.

Christmas had come and gone. Now, three weeks into 1980, Nima and Grover were busier than ever wrapping up the Darien job. They were aiming for a roof-raising party the second week in February because Grover had scheduled a new job in Westport the middle of February. But this time it would be without Nima. He would be gone by then. This would undoubtedly bother Nima a lot more than when he had left Mr. Mastroberadino's class three nights earlier.

The last evening of class, Nima had gotten into the car with a certificate that proved he had successfully completed the course. On the way home he was exceptionally quiet. Usually Nima was full of interesting gossip that he had picked up during the coffee breaks. But just before I turned onto River Road, Nima said that his teacher told him he was really going to miss having him in the class because he had been one of the best students. Nima's voice was strained and soft as he told me that Salvatore cried when they said good-bye.

By the following morning Nima had perked up. In fact, he had perked up enough to Xerox six copies of his English-as-a-Second-Language certificate. One was for Grover, one for Judd, one for Lhakpa, and one for us. The only person who didn't get one was Mingma. That was because he got *two*—just in case he felt like giving one to Pasang.

As I addressed the envelope to Mingma, Nima told me why he hadn't given his teacher the going-away present he had taken to class. He also told me what it was. I thought to myself it was a blessing in disguise that Mr. Mastroberadino had been spared the gift.

The afternoon of his class Nima and Grover had been running errands in Westport. While Grover was depositing $3,245 and withdrawing $200, Nima ran across the street to Dorain Drugs to look for a gift. But once he got inside he couldn't decide what to get. Finally a saleslady came over and asked if she could help. Nima told her that he was looking for something on sale and under five dollars. The lady pointed him toward a rack of sale items. It was there he found the perfect gift: a Bugs Bunny lunch pail with matching thermos. It had been reduced from $8.99 to $4.29. Nima said that Mr. Mastroberadino always carried an apple and a jar of Sanka in a brown paper bag for the coffee break.

But when Nima got to class, he noticed that none of the other students had gifts. He didn't want them to look "cheap like Khambas," so he brought the gift back home. He was going to give it to John, to carry his pencils, books, and coffee when he went to New York.

A week after Nima completed his English course, he began First Aid. Originally, I had intended to enroll him in a Red Cross first aid course. But after a long discussion with one of the instructors, I realized their course was much too advanced for Nima. And the types of first aid they covered would be useless to Nima back in the Himalayas. He needed things pertinent to the region, such as what to do for the all-too-common kukri knife-cut, a broken bone from a fall, burns from an open-pit fire, frostbite, snakebites, and dog bites from the terrifying Tibetan mastiff. And he would have to use implements that were available. Of course there was so much Nima couldn't do, in spite of what we could teach him. I thought back to Day Four of our trek, as we were camped on the shelf of a mountain.

We had finished dinner early, and there was still daylight. I became aware that a frail-looking woman was approaching us, several children with her. Her eyes were sad and expressive. She was wearing a dark shawl over her head. She pressed her hands in front of her face, and said the usual namaste. We returned her bow with the same greeting.

She tried to communicate with us in Nepalese and gestures, almost frantically. There were tears welling in her eyes. We couldn't understand anything she was saying, and waved to Nima to join us. As he translated, we learned that her husband was desperately ill, that he was in great pain, voiding blood in both urine and feces. Didn't we have any Sahib medicine that she could give him? From the description, it seemed obvious that only a hospital could supply and sort of care for this. But the only real hospital was in Kathmandu, days away even if he could be carried there on the back of a porter.

With our medical kit gone, there was practically nothing we could do. But she continued to beseech us, bursting into a full flood of tears. "Was there nothing, however small, we could give her to try?" Nima translated her question. The situation seemed hopeless, but perhaps some of our remaining medicine, I was thinking, could at least provide a placebo effect and help the wife feel that she was doing everything possible.

John went to our duffel bags and brought out two anti-diarrhea tablets, four of the remaining aspirins, and a tiny sample bottle of cough syrup that had survived the theft. We had Nima explain when to take them. Then she went off quickly with her children to administer them. I wondered if it weren't the wrong thing to do, because the medicine might give her false hope. But then I thought that any action is better than standing by hopelessly and doing nothing.

Within half an hour, the wife was back with a dishpan, explaining to Nima what was happening to her husband. The pan was nearly full of crimson, clotted blood. The husband was obviously hemorrhaging beyond the scope of any modern medicine. We told her through Nima how terribly sorry we felt and how we wished we could do more. After our robbery, we could not even offer money.

She nodded at last, in deep resignation and sorrow. Then she told Nima she wanted to thank us, anyway. She drew two eggs from a pocket in her apron, bowed, and offered them to us with both hands.

In the few moments I stood there facing the woman, I thought about how fragile life was. I thought maybe the Sherpas' belief that all life is an illusion is the only way to survive personal tragedy. The Sherpa Buddhist actually lives for the moment of death, because it is not death but birth. The Western world, for the most part, lives to avoid death. By not fearing death, the Sherpas seem to have a greater zest and love for life. But to them, death is the greater reality, in contrast to the fragmentary and impermanent world of illusion we live in now.

John asked Nima to thank the woman for the eggs and to refuse with our deep appreciation. She shook her head and insisted we keep them. I took the gift and headed back toward our tent when I suddenly remembered that I had found extra aspirin in my parka. I ran to catch the woman to give her the medicine. She had stopped in front of the Sherpas' tent. As I approached I noticed Nima passing her a fifty-rupee note—a full two days' pay. The money was to hire a porter to carry her husband to the Kathmandu hospital.

I went to bed that night with a sense of wonderment and reverance for the human race.

Back in America, I had a different sense of wonderment as to how Nima would fare in his first aid training. The Red Cross suggested a few emergency medical technicians in our area who might be willing to give Nima private instructions. The EMT turned out to be Sue Adler, a friend, a neighbor, and—most important—a person endowed with infinite patience and a good sense of humor. During Sue's first visit to our house she spoke to Nima about what types of things he would need to learn. By the time she left, she felt certain that she needed additional troops. She decided on Kathy McAuliff, a registered nurse and also another very patient human being.

During his training Nima proved nimble, sprightly, and totally unpredictable. One of us would drop on the lawn like a wounded mountaineer and simulate everything from a broken leg to a snake bite. Nima would invariably decide on the wrong treatment. I told Nima that I couldn't believe he could be such a quick study at carpentry and English and so bad in grasping first aid. His only comment was that just the thought of blood made him feel queasy, and that snake bites reminded him of what the lama had told him many years earlier. "Nima, if you're not a good boy you're coming back in your next life as a snake."

During one lesson, "Deep Wounds and Cuts," we just couldn't get Nima to pay attention. Out of frustration, I ran to the house, doused my arm with tomato catsup, and then returned, screaming that I was bleeding to death. Nima took one look at the "blood" and took off toward the house. Sue and Kathy overtook him and dragged him back to the river. They began instructing him on how to clean my wound with ice-cold river water.

Meanwhile, the same neighbor who had phoned months earlier wanting to know why Nima was riding his bike precariously close to the river now wanted to know if she could call Weston's EMT. She said that they could be at our house in three minutes and have me at the Norwalk Hospital in fifteen. John, who took the call, calmly told her that if she observed closely she would recognize one of the Weston's EMTs in our backyard. The neighbor left the phone, came to the edge of the river, and said nothing further.

When Sue reached the category of frostbite, Nima

graphically revealed how it was treated on the icy slopes of Ama Dablam. He placed his left hand on the ground and simulated a meat cutter with his right. He brought the edge of his right hand down over the unsuspecting fingers of his left and accompanied it with vivid sound effects. "Chop-Chung!"

Nima had a lot to learn, but after six lessons, three tins of Band-Aids, and innumerable rolls of bandages and elastic tape, we had to leave him to the mercy of Buddha and what little knowledge had entered through the pores. For time was short. In less than nine days Nima would be boarding the Air India flight for his return trip home.

Nima planned on quitting his job with Grover so he could have his last three days in America free. That was something he could afford to do. The wad was now up to $1,464, not counting a piggy bank full of coins. And that brought up another point: Nima was still stubbornly refusing to put his money into travelers checks.

But John was equally stubborn. The crisis came when Nima tried to prove he could safely carry back the wads of tens and twenties in his knapsack. With a great deal of showmanship, he brought a roll of Bounty paper towels to the dining room table and proceeded to demonstrate. He unrolled a generous length of toweling along the table, placing the wad of bills beside it. Carefully, he peeled off a twenty, waved it in the air, and then stuck it far back into the roll. One by one, he pushed the bills into the roll of towels and then made them disappear. It was the sloppiest roll of paper towels I had ever seen. I could hardly believe Nima was serious.

Nima explained his reasoning: no one would ever think of stealing a roll of extra-absorbent Bounty paper towels. I told Nima that the Bounty towels looked suspicious. And what would happen when he went through customs in New Delhi? The customs officer would see the roll of paper towels, unwind it, and find the bills. If the official had slippery hands, Nima could kiss the wad good-bye. Or what if the customs man assumed Nima was doing something illegal, a very logical assumption. Maybe he would think Nima was trafficking in drugs. He wouldn't give Nima a chance to explain that he just liked the feel of a wad. Nima would be thrown in the slammer, never to be heard from again. As my worst-scenario argument reached a climax, my voice got louder for effect. I wound it up by telling Nima that his was the stupidest idea I had ever heard.

John made no such value judgment. He simply went to the kitchen phone, called the bank manager at the Union Trust, and set up an appointment for nine o'clock the next morning. John, Nima, and I could come in and hear directly from a banker how wise it would be to convert the cash to travelers checks.

Nima's last day of work coincided with the Darien roof-raising party. This was no accident. Grover said that there was no way he could say good-bye to one without the other. Even though the job wouldn't be officially completed for several more days, the party was pushed ahead to meet Nima's deadline.

The roof-raising party was over by four-thirty, and by five o'clock Grover and Nima pulled into our driveway just as they had during the last four and a half months. And just as predictably Grover used our house as a combination office-pub. He dragged in his leather briefcase, placed it on the bar, and shuffled through various papers, got out his pocket computor, helped himself to something, and then got down to the business of his phone calls. Nima, meanwhile, was making popcorn for their snack.

When I heard Grover and Nima in the kitchen, I dreaded going downstairs. This evening would mark Nima's last day on Grover's payroll, and more important, as Grover's sidekick. For the last four months Nima had lived and breathed Grover Mills. Now his stint as apprentice carpenter was over. Although Nima never verbalized how much he was going to miss working with Grover, he didn't have to. Little things had crept into his conversation that indicated just how tough this was going to be. In fact, at breakfast that morning he had mumbled something about hoping Grover would have a chance to swing by Fairfield Lumber so he could say "so long" to Stubby and Ray. When he said that, everything inside of me wanted to tell him to stay forever. But everything outside of me said that this was impossible. Nima had to make his own life. He had his own family and his own culture.

But when I got downstairs that afternoon, I was surprised. Nima was not in the dumps. He was in the kitchen, popping popcorn, going through a skit of the time Grover sent him to look for the fifteen-light French door. As Nima was acting out all the characters and imitating the voices, Grover sounded like a one-man laugh track. I had to hand it to Nima: he did have a knack for recreating scenes and catching specific characteristics.

Nima spotted me beside Grover and stopped the French-door skit.

"Memsahib," he said, "popcorns?"

"Sure. So how was the roof-raising bash?" I asked.

"Good parties!" Nima seemed to have had an even better time at the roof-raising party than at the English-class party. It was probably because he had a closer camaraderie with Grover and his men than with his fellow students. He related specific incidents from the time the party started until it ended. Of course it was all inside stuff. You had to work with Grover to understand what was so funny about Harold not letting anyone put drinks on his precious table saw, or the precut studs that arrived a quarter of an inch too short, or the time Mike almost fell through an open skylight.

After Grover made four phone calls, quenched his thirst, and scooped the popcorn bowl clean, he went out to his pickup. Suddenly I saw his briefcase on the bar and ran out to give it to him. It was then that Grover told me what had happened with Nima on the way home.

Grover said that for the past week Nima had the "thousand-mile stare." He had hoped Nima would talk about his leaving, but Nima never did. Several times Grover subtly asked what Nima was going to do when he got back to Phakding. Nima just shook his head. But then at the party Nima rejoined the living. He seemed to enjoy himself as much as everyone else.

On the way home, Nima's mood plummeted. It was then that Grover told Nima he knew how hard it was for him to leave. When he and Kerrie were in the Peace Corps in Chile they made good friends, and leaving was the hardest thing they ever had to do. But, Grover told Nima, if they hadn't left Chile, he would have not gone into construction and would not have started Grover Mills Construction. He suggested that if Nima didn't go home, he would never build the Nima Dorje Sherpa Teahouse of Phakding. And that would really disappoint Grover, because he had steered Nima's whole apprenticeship toward making that teahouse a reality.

Grover's words seemed to have helped. The last thing Nima ever wanted to be was a disappointment to Grover. That night, after Grover left, Nima seemed more determined than ever to go back to Phakding and put into practice everything he had learned.

Meanwhile we were getting together a surprise party on Sunday evening for Nima. But before Nima went to bed that night, I decided not to keep it a secret any longer. And I was glad I didn't. When I told Nima about it, his thirty-two-tooth grin made us all feel better.

All of Nima's friends delighted in the idea of a going-away party. But nobody was more delighted than Nima. The day of the party, while I was cooking, Nima cleaned the house from top to bottom, decorated the living room with fifty percent more crêpe paper and balloons than necessary, and arranged and rearranged the paper hats, cups, and plates. I argued with Nima over paper hats, but in the end he won out. Then at six o'clock he got on his alpine outfit, complete with mountain-climbing boots.

At seven, the guests began arriving, all bearing gifts. And Nima was bearing that Christmas look again. After everyone arrived, I brought out the special cake I had ordered. It was a cake baked in the approximate shape of Mount Everest, with white frosting and a little mountain climber scaling the peak. Nima didn't react to the cake quite the way I thought he would. First, he couldn't believe it *was* a cake. I convinced him by making him run his index finger along one side and then taste it. But he still seemed surprised that anyone would actually eat something that looked so good.

Several bottles of wine, two trays of lasagne, and half a cake later, Nima led us in Sherpa dances while John played the piano. Later came the best part of the evening—for Nima anyway: he opened his gifts. He felt obliged to give about ten minutes of lip service to every gift he unwrapped. He admired each present from all possible angles, commenting all the while on just how perfect it was. Then he thanked the giver for everthing they had ever done for him.

Nima had a memory bank like an Apple home computer. His thank-you speeches were reminiscent of Oscar night at the Dorothy Chandler Pavilion. John kept giving Nima signals to wrap it up and get on to the next gift, but Nima had the floor and he wasn't about to give it up.

He spent the longest time on Grover, thanking him for everything from the time he saved his life down at the dump, to all the times Grover detoured past Baskin-Robbins. Among others, he thanked Arlene Skutch, my art teacher, for the Cross pen and for taking him to the Metropolitan Museum of Art and the World Trade Towers for lunch. Then he reminisced with Arlene about the time he helped her take her dog, Mister, to the vet, and how surprised he was to see a whole hospital just for animals. He thanked Dorothy Thau for all the times she picked him up and dropped him off at Staples, and all the times after class they stopped at Dameon's for ice cream and coffee. He thanked Sue Adler, his first aid instructor, and her husband, Danny, for the money belt and the ten bucks inside it. And of course he reminded Sue of the time he thought the catsup on my arm was blood. He reminded Danny of all the "excellent" lunches Sue had made for them, and all the times Danny was called out to deliver babies and Nima had to finish his lunch. He thanked the Blinns for the airplane wings and his visit to the 747. Ironically, he didn't mention their daughter, Nancy.

We drove Nima to the JFK Airport at four in the afternoon. In the trunk were his three duffel bags and one backpack. On the Merritt Parkway, we didn't say much. As John drove, I dropped my head back again to a year earlier when we had said good-bye to Nima at Lukla airstrip on his home ground. The scene of Nima placing the garlands around our necks reflected in a single instance the kindness and love of the Sherpa people. This matter-of-fact kindness had been evident all along the trail: the extravagant hospitality of the Sherpas, where there was so little to give; the Spirit doctor of Khumjung, who came down the trail from his village in the deep snow to try to help two strangers he had never seen before; the poignant and grateful look of the mother with the badly burned child; Nima's mother, who stayed up half the night to prepare a Sherpa feast for her son's two American friends; Nima, who had given two days' pay for the sick woman's husband to be carried to a Kathmandu hospital.

Without being aware of it, we had found the meaning of Truth all through our long journey—Nima's smile in the face of his illness; the monks' endless chanting while the prayer wheels spun, sending prayers for peace and compassion out on the winds to the rest of the world; the singing of the porters and children on the trail. Each person had his own truth, including ourselves. But the reflections we found there shone back at us and aided in a self-realization for which we would be grateful forever. We had reached our Everest spiritually, if not physically.

Now, with Nima heading back to his high mountain home, it was time for another good-bye. I pictured our meeting with Nima at JFK six months earlier. He was a walking skeleton. Now in the back seat of the car he was round and robust. But would he stay that way? According to Dr. Altbaum, if he continued to take his medicine for the next six months, he had a very good chance of a full recovery.

Two days earlier, I had taken Nima to Dr. Altbaum's office to pick up his chest X rays and say "so long." Dr. Altbaum, a thirty-four-year-old who looked as if he would have no trouble scrambling around the mountains, handed

Nima a large manila envelope containing his vital medical records. As he did so, they embraced. Both had tears in their eyes. Usually Nima was full of interesting construction anecdotes for Dr. Altbaum. Not this time. Nima was silent. As we walked out of the familiar reception office, Nima turned to me and said that he had dreamed just the evening before that Dr. Altbaum would go to Nepal on a trekking expedition. I asked Nima if he told that to Dr. Altbaum. Nima said no, it was only a dream.

In the soft light of the airport restaurant, we watched the planes take off and land in the distance. Other planes in the foreground poked their sides into the ramp bellows, their tails rising like enormous shark fins, two stories high. We were all strangely quiet. Even Nima seemed stiff and un-communicative. None of us felt much like eating. John spent several minutes spinning the olive in his drink. I swirled the red wine in my glass. Nima chewed on the straw in his Coke. Everything that had to be said had been said already.

We didn't hear the flight announced, but we were sure it was time. We walked toward the check-in counter. There was a crowd and there was no use in going farther. Nima turned suddenly toward us, dropped his hand baggage, and embraced each of us in turn. Then he moved up to join the passengers and in seconds was gulped up by the crowd. We tried to wave to him, but even that was useless.

We walked toward the parking lot and over the same pedestrian ramp Nima had struggled across so many months before. I could almost hear his first words when he hit the Connecticut thruway. "Many car. Many peoples. Many house." Now he would probably say, "Hey man, dig all the cars."

# AFTERWORD

$\gamma r \cdot \prec$

If Nima had any adjustments to make when he went back to the mountains, we also had our own to make in Weston. Several weeks after Nima left, a letter arrived, dictated to his friend from Kathmandu.

Dear Sir John and Elizabeth—Daily Namaste—
How are you for moment? My journey from USA to Nepal was very enjoyable time. It was no problems about to get money in Nepal. My USA visit time was like dream. I never ever forget about your hospitality and great help for my health. Thank you very, very much for everything you done for me.

Well now I am leaving for trekking to Everest base camp, Gokyo etc. But still I feel very sad and lonely to leave USA and all of you. I always thinking about my beautiful time with you.

Now the money I am going to make a teahouse in my village. I dream Memsahib and Sahib come stay in teahouse. In 2 week time I be with family in Phakding and give cloth and money.

Is it possible to send TB tablet a bit earlier it will be great full for me. Because, in summer season I will be staying in Khumbu, also I have to leave Kathmandu about after a month. Now I go to bed it is 10 PM.

Have good time and reply me soon. Well I am waiting for you kindness reply. Good night for today. Many loves to you.

Please to tell of my namaste to all our friends. Mingma happy for cow hat.

Namaste
Your friend, Nima Dorje Sherpa

It was three months later before we heard from Nima again. His letter was full of good news. The medicine we sent him had arrived. Nima was as healthy as the day he left. If his first letter had sounded sad and lonely, his second letter was filled with nothing but exuberance, so much so that I felt a twinge of jealousy. He seemed to be adapting just fine without us. And he had every reason to be so optimistic. In the last month, he had been promoted from junior Sherpa guide to sirdar.

This not only meant a twenty-five-percent increase in salary, but a prestige that went far beyond *any* amount of money.

By the time Thanksgiving arrived we had received two more letters. In each, Nima reminisced about his visit. He wanted to know about everything. He even asked if we ever got Peter Kunkel to fix our dripping kitchen faucet, or if Stubby down at Fairfield Lumber ever found the Teco joist hangers. Nima would end each letter thanking us for everything we had done for him and reminding us that in just one more year he should have his teahouse completed. He was hoping we would return to Nepal and be his guests for as long as we wanted.

Several days after Christmas, two gifts arrived from Kathmandu. Nima sent Tibetan costume boots for me and a wool hat and gloves for John. We placed the colorful gifts around the tree. Although nearly a year had passed since Nima left, we still missed his buoyant spirit—and his neatly wrapped gifts of Morton salt and Hostess Ding Dongs.

During the following year Nima continued to write whenever possible, giving us all the latest news on his family and the progress on his teahouse. His youngest brother was starting school. His sister had gotten married, which set his father back a few "big ones." But his father had acquired two more yaks and was taking on more trading expeditions into Tibet to pay for the three-day wedding ceremony. His mother was getting "older and stronger" with every year. I still found it hard to get used to Nima boasting about how old his mother was.

The only time Nima seemed to complain was when it came to his teahouse. "Very difficult to chop wood without Black and Decker," he wrote. In addition to this news, he mentioned how he was putting to use the first aid course. "While I was in Khumbu I did some first aid, I bought some bandages, some antibiotic cream and savlon [sic] etc. from Kathmandu and I treat quite a few patients with small cut, infected wounds, scabis [sic] etc. Those scabis cream from USA was very useful and helpful. I distribute them for scabis patients, and they recover very well."

Finally, we got word that Nima had completed his teahouse. It also looked as if Nima's single life was coming to an end. He wrote: "I am going to marry in coming December because I need helper for running the teahouse and to look after my old parents." But in Nima's next letter he said that the wedding was off. He never said why. He did, however, say that his sister and her husband would be running the teahouse so he would be free to lead treks and expeditions.

*Many months after Nima returned to the Himalayas, he finally completed his teahouse. Nima's mother,* center, *proudly poses with village friends.*

The very latest news we received on Nima came second hand. One day in early spring the phone rang. It was Robert Adair, a man who lives about twenty minutes from us in Connecticut. He had just returned from a trek in Nepal where Nima had been sirdar. The man said that on the first day of the trek Nima asked him where he was from. Assuming that Nima would have never heard of Connecticut, he merely said, "I am from the United States." Nima promptly replied, "Sir, the United States is very big. Where in the United States do you live?"

Again assuming that Nima could never know his state, he answered by saying that he lived very close to a place called

New York City. Hearing that, Nima said, "Sir, New York City is very big. Many big buildings and good restaurants, good stores. But where do you live?"

Robert Adair was a little taken aback by Nima's knowledge of the world, but he still answered Nima indirectly. "Nima, I live in a very beautiful state where there are lots of trees and old houses. It is called Con-nec-ti-cut." As he was carefully breaking down each syllable, Nima was nodding his head as Sherpas often do, taking in every word and expression. Finally, when the man completed his Sesame Street description of where he lived, Nima said rather casually, "Sir, you must live very close to Peter's Market on Route 57 in Weston."

This is how I will remember Nima the best—always the unexpected. I have no idea what Nima's next letter will bring. I am almost afraid to speculate. Knowing Nima, he could do anything from franchising out a string of his teahouses to starting up his own talk show. I do, however, feel as if I can count on one thing: wherever Nima goes and whomever he comes in contact with, he will charm and pleasantly confuse their lives as much as he did ours.

# CHRISTIAN HERALD ASSOCIATION AND ITS MINISTRIES

**CHRISTIAN HERALD ASSOCIATION,** founded in 1878, publishes The Christian Herald Magazine, one of the leading interdenominational religious monthlies in America. Through its wide circulation, it brings inspiring articles and the latest news of religious developments to many families. From the magazine's pages came the initiative for CHRISTIAN HERALD CHILDREN and THE BOWERY MISSION, two individually supported not-for-profit corporations.

**CHRISTIAN HERALD CHILDREN,** established in 1894, is the name for a unique and dynamic ministry to disadvantaged children, offering hope and opportunities which would not otherwise be available for reasons of poverty and neglect. The goal is to develop each child's potential and to demonstrate Christian compassion and understanding to children in need.

*Mont Lawn* is a permanent camp located in Bushkill, Pennsylvania. It is the focal point of a ministry which provides a healthful "vacation with a purpose" to children who without it would be confined to the streets of the city. Up to 1000 children between the age of 7 and 11 come to Mont Lawn each year.

Christian Herald Children maintains year-round contact with children by means of a *City Youth Ministry.* Central to its philosophy is the belief that only through sustained relationships and demonstrated concern can individual lives be truly enriched. Special emphasis is on individual guidance, spiritual and family counseling and tutoring. This follow-up ministry to inner-city children culminates for many in financial assistance toward higher education and career counseling.

**THE BOWERY MISSION,** located at 227 Bowery, New York City, has since 1879 been reaching out to the lost men on the Bowery, offering them what could be their last chance to rebuild their lives. Every man is fed, clothed and ministered to. Countless numbers have entered the 90-day residential rehabilitation program at the Bowery Mission. A concentrated ministry of counseling, medical care, nutrition therapy, Bible study and Gospel services awakens a man to spiritual renewal within himself.

These ministries are supported solely by the voluntary contributions of individuals and by legacies and bequests. Contributions are tax deductible. Checks should be made out either to CHRISTIAN HERALD CHILDREN or to THE BOWERY MISSION.

**Administrative Office: 40 Overlook Drive, Chappaqua, New York 10514**
**Telephone: (914) 769-9000**